D1360318

SAVING AMERICA

The True Story of How a Gym Owner and a Man From the Ghetto Helped Save Our Republic

BY

JOSH BARNETT
&
DAVID JOSE

SAVING AMERICA

Ordering Information: Quantity sales. Special discounts are available on quantity purchases by corporations, associations, and others. Orders by U.S. trade bookstores and wholesalers.

DREAMSTARTERS

www.DreamStartersPublishing.com

Table of Contents

Introduction.. 4

The Corruption of CPS.. 9

Understanding Medical Kidnapping.............................25

The Importance of Education.......................................40

Working Toward Legislative Change 71

Defending Against Other Forms of Government Overreach..........87

Returning the Power to the People............................ 111

Conclusion.. 128

Photo Gallery.. 131

CONTACT PAGE... 134

Introduction

What you are about to read will shock you. This is not meant to scare you. It is simply meant to open your eyes to what is really happening in the world and provide you the tools on how to fight back against corruption. Buckle up patriots, because we are in for a wild ride.

The light shines in the darkness, and the darkness has not overcome it.

John 1:5

Child Protective Services (CPS) and similar government organizations claim to be dedicated to the welfare of children. They are meant to be services that work to protect kids, and that families in Arizona and across the country can trust. However, recently the general public's faith in CPS and similar institutions has been shaken as a result of corruption that is putting children in danger, and this corruption is no conspiracy theory. It is a widespread and serious issue that's resulted in the separation of young children from loving homes, and it is exactly what Josh Barnett and David Jose are working so hard to prevent.

Our story begins in late 2019, in the office of Arizona Senator David Farnsworth. Senator Farnsworth held an open meeting to shine a light on recent allegations of the significant corruption of CPS. In particular, he was concerned about reports that CPS was taking custody of hundreds of kids each year without proper documentation of why these children were removed from their homes and where they ended up after they were taken into custody. Their records were wiped after six months, which meant there was little accountability for how these children were being treated after being taken from their parents. Worse, the allegations also include reports from concerned parents that CPS wasn't just taking kids out of genuinely abusive situations, but removing them from loving families without following proper procedures. These stories came from concerned parents and family members, including one attendee of the meeting, David Jose.

CPS attempted to take custody of David's own kids, claiming there was abuse and neglect when in reality there was none. CPS did not have the proper evidence to take his kids into custody; on the contrary, they acted on the pretense of a lie spread by his step-daughter rather than thoroughly checking for problems themselves. David had evidence to refute these allegations, but it was largely ignored and brushed under the rug by CPS. This experience opened David's eyes to the reality of the corruption that has allowed CPS to engage in so-called "legal kidnappings" of children, and it is what brought him to the meeting in Senator

Farnsworth's office to demand that something be done to prevent other families from losing their children.

Meanwhile, Josh Barnett attended the meeting as a congressional candidate looking to listen to community concerns. He wanted to get involved with the people of Arizona and understand what he could do to help them should he be elected. It was here that Josh was first introduced to the problems with CPS and legal kidnapping, specifically through hearing David speak about his own experiences. David was deeply knowledgeable about relevant laws, and it was clear he was well informed in matters of child welfare.

After an introduction through Evelyn Keiling, a mutual friend, Josh and David knew they were meant to work together to fight back against CPS taking kids without following due process. Since then, they have continued to work together to not only help parents get their kids back when the children should never have been taken in the first place, but also to inform parents across the nation about the dangers of legal kidnapping, as well as what they can do to protect themselves and their families.

CPS, like many other government institutions, started out as a program to protect families. However, over the years it has morphed into a service puppeted by greed and misconduct. While it is necessary for social workers to intervene in cases where children really are being abused or neglected, we cannot allow the continued abduction of kids from homes without any evidence of abuse, only fueled by flimsy allegations. According to "Arizona Juvenile CourtsTerminating Parental Rights by Jury Trial in Arizona: A First Year Look May 2005", in 2003, CPS had due process in the courts (for one year) and only 13% of kids were removed from the home. This meant that 87% of the other cases had their children sent back to their homes due to frivolous or other nonsensical reasons. After due process was taken away from CPS courts (after 2003), 151 of 158 completed bench trials resulted in judges' rulings severing parental rights on all or some of the children resulting in over 95.5% of children are taken from parents and it has become a $1,000,000,000 industry in Arizona. It went from 13% with due process to almost 96% without due process that the kids were taken away from the parents and put into the CPS system to become part of the money making program. We cannot let kids continue to be traumatized by the actions of CPS, nor can we allow CPS to get away with having little to no accountability for what methods are used to remove kids from their families or what happens to them after they are taken into custody. In short, we cannot allow government organizations to operate as tyrannical kings with no opposition, especially when it is harming families and kids. We must protect children, whether this means pushing back against corruption in CPS or asserting our rights as parents to keep our kids healthy and happy in the face of mask mandates and unlawful quarantine closures which threaten our livelihoods and our ability to provide for our families. Just like our ancestors during the Revolutionary War, we must stand up for our rights against those who would threaten them, and save America by fighting for our convictions.

In *Saving America*, you'll learn the ways in which government corruption threatens families across Arizona and the rest of the country. You'll develop a better understanding of what CPS is and isn't allowed to do so that you can better protect your family. You'll learn how you can inspire change in your own community and contribute to the movement. You'll also learn what tools you have at your disposal for fighting corruption in all its forms, and how you can implement them to fight back against unjust regulations through contacting your representatives and declaring your rights.

In the fight against legal kidnapping, the best weapon you have is knowledge. It is only by staying informed that you can push back against government overreach and make a difference. Protect your kids and advocate for change to ensure that corruption never tears apart another family again.

Chapter 1

The Corruption of CPS

"The Pledge of Allegiance reflects the truth that faith in God has played a significant role in American since the days of the founding of our country."

Randy Neugebauer

No good parent should have to worry about a single call taking away their children. However, with the current state of CPS, there is a very real chance that a false allegation is all it takes to separate you from your child. Of course, CPS wasn't always such a corrupt service, but recent laws have given its workers greater power and greater reason to take custody of as many kids as possible, rather than looking for real evidence of abuse. The primary reason why there is so much corruption today is that taking custody of kids is no longer about protecting them; instead, it is about making money.

There are, to be sure, good social workers with no intention of splitting up happy families. Despite this, the bad apples have spoiled the whole bunch, turning CPS into a service that parents can no longer trust to look into allegations thoroughly and prove them innocent of any false claims. If you have CPS called on you but you know you love and care for your children just fine, your initial assumption would likely be that you should have no issues, but this simply isn't the case. More and more, everyday parents are finding themselves locked in battles with the state to argue for custody of their own kids despite doing nothing to prompt their removal. Even though it is CPS instigating these long court battles, it is the families and especially the children who suffer for them, and the CPS workers who rake in the money for these unjustified kidnappings.

The real reason for the sharp rise in legal kidnappings stems from laws that effectively encourage them, even providing a monetary award to CPS workers who successfully separate kids from their parents, regardless of whether they are actually putting the kids in safer environments or not. In particular, there are two main laws that allow for and enable legal kidnapping. These are Title 42 and the Adoption and Safe Families Act.

Title 42

Title 42 refers to the 42 U.S. Code. It is a law related to social welfare and public health, and covers a wide range of issues including reducing the spread of communicable diseases and supporting social services. More specifically, Chapter 67 of Title 42 deals with "Child abuse prevention and treatment and adoption reform," and it is this law that has enabled the majority of the corruption that now plagues CPS. This is because of Chapter 67 Subchapter III, which establishes "community-based grants for the prevention of child abuse and neglect" (Legal Information Institute, n.d., para. 1). In theory, this doesn't sound too bad, but in practice, this law allows government officials to profit off of cases where CPS takes custody of kids.

The grants provided by Title 42 are intended for "financing the start-up, maintenance, expansion, or redesign of specific community-based child abuse and neglect prevention program services" (Legal Information Institute, n.d., para. 15). While the majority of these grants should go toward prevention and education programs meant to support families and provide them with resources to eliminate the potential causes behind abuse and neglect like drug addictions and untreated mental illnesses, this money rarely reaches its intended targets. Instead, when children are taken by CPS, payments are made to the state. These payments then get funneled into the pockets of corrupt government officials and CPS workers, meaning that for every kid who is legally kidnapped, those involved get a payout.

This system incentivizes CPS employees to remove kids from homes even when it is not in the children's best interests. To make as much money as possible, CPS needs to take custody of as many kids as possible. This leads them to pursue false flags and ignore evidence that doesn't support their point of view. Instead of supporting healthy families and caring about protecting child welfare, the system becomes corrupt, and more and more kids are separated from their parents.

There are many ways for CPS to orchestrate the unjust removal of a child from their home. One especially notable one is the falsification of drug test results. Many parents who have submitted to drug tests knowing they were not on drugs somehow ended up with positive results, which would indicate to a court that the home is not fit for a child. The courts use refer parents to the states drug testing company to, once again, make another side profit off the people. The programs used by the state for drug testing, psychiatric testing, and counseling are all part of the money making scheme because the parents are not allowed to pick their own, 3rd party, testers. It is mandated that they use the courts referrals only. These fabrications can then be used to increase the number of children taken into custody by CPS in a year, further increasing payouts. While this sounds like a nightmare, it's very real; a 2020 investigation of falsified drug reports in Indiana uncovered the truth about voided screens, which occur "when the person who's supposed to take the drug test fails to show up. That information goes to the court and can be considered a positive test and used against a parent or guardian," (Chapman, 2020, para. 14) even if there is no way to confirm that the parent was on drugs at the time. Because of this, it may be in your best interest to refuse a drug test depending on your situation, even if you know you are not taking drugs. If you do submit to a test, be sure to keep the appointment to reduce the risk of the voided screen being submitted as a positive test result.

In addition to Title 42, one other law is notable for encouraging CPS to take kids from their homes unnecessarily with a financial reward for doing so. This is The Adoption and Safe Families Act.

The Adoption and Safe Families Act

The Adoption and Safe Families Act is a law passed in 1997 that was enacted during the Clinton administration, after receiving congressional approval. According to this act, "reasonable efforts to preserve and reunify the family shall not be required on behalf of certain parents," including those who CPS deems "pose a serious risk to a child's health or safety" (Congress.gov, 1997, para. 8). While the act is intended to promote additional safety measures for keeping kids out of homes with abusive and dangerous guardians, the wording of the act is open to interpretation. It isn't specified what can be considered a serious risk to a child's safety, which allows bad faith actors to define the law as they see fit and prevent kids who have been taken by CPS from reuniting with their families.

In fact, CPS employees are encouraged to keep families separated for at least one year, and there are incentives available for those who place children in permanent homes other than those of their birth parents or previous legal guardians. The Act authorizes the Secretary of Health and Human Services to "award an adoption incentive grant to an incentive-eligible State meeting specified criteria whose number of foster child or special needs adoptions for a fiscal year exceeds a base number calculated according to a specified formula" (Congress.gov, 1997, para. 14). In other words, states create quotas for how many kids they need to place in foster homes in a year to get their grants, which means corrupt CPS employees will attempt to keep kids away from their families rather than making reasonable efforts to return them to their parents. Just like Title 42, this law

14

incentivizes the separation of families, regardless of whether or not there is truly a justifiable reason for doing so. These payouts lead CPS workers to value money over the well-being of children and their families.

How Children Are Taken From Their Parents Against Their Wishes

While some cases of CPS taking kids are legal despite not being fully justified, other cases are in violation of the law, though most parents don't know this and thus aren't able to argue their case effectively. This is because CPS frequently does not follow the proper procedures when taking kids. Notably, except for in certain cases, CPS cannot take children without the consent of the parents. Legally, "CPS can only remove your child if they have a court order or if the child is an emergency situation," which means they must investigate claims of abuse personally and thoroughly and find that "the home is not safe for the child, the child is in imminent danger or an emergency has made it impossible for them to leave the child at home" (Thelin, 2021, para. 6-7). If CPS cannot confirm any of these things to be true, then they are not allowed to take your kids unless you consent to it. If CPS takes children under false pretenses without parental consent, there is a good chance that you can fight back, but only if you are aware that the law offers you this protection.

SAVING AMERICA

As a parent, it is important to be aware of your rights when it comes to CPS so you can point out potential violations of these rights when they occur. First, know that while CPS is legally required to investigate all claims, you have a right to be informed of any claims made against you during the investigation. Additionally, while social workers can show up at your home unannounced, you must be present at the home in order for them to conduct the investigation to ensure no evidence is planted or fabricated. You must also give consent for them to enter, and they cannot force their way inside without a court order. You have a right to request an interpreter if there is a language barrier between you and the CPS case workers. While CPS may ask personal or invasive questions, you have a right to remain silent, as you do with any legal proceedings, and you can invoke it at any time. CPS cannot require you to submit to a drug test without a court order. If they pursue criminal charges, you have a right to an attorney, even if you cannot afford to pay for one yourself. However, if you can afford it, it's a good idea to seek out a lawyer who has experience in CPS cases so you get the best possible representation. You should also research any state laws that may add additional restrictions on what CPS is allowed to do in your area, whether you are preparing your case or if you simply want to stay informed.

Note that, while you have rights, the law also permits CPS to do certain things that you may not initially realize. For example, CPS can speak to your child without your permission and without you being present. This means they may talk to your child at school or at a doctor's office or hospital. Any conversations you or your child have with CPS can be used in any legal proceedings, and they are not considered to be confidential, so don't offer up unnecessary information. Still, while it's possible for CPS to press criminal charges, this is relatively very rare, and you generally have nothing to worry about if you know you are not harming your child.

A Lack of Arrests

While any parent who has had their child taken from them unjustly knows just how terrible CPS corruption is, the movement has its critics. Some people argue that CPS is only taking children out of homes where they are unsafe, and that any time CPS takes custody of a child, they are saving that child. This is, of course, what everyone hopes is the case when CPS gets involved. Ideally, no children would ever be taken from homes where they have a loving family who wants them to live safe, happy lives. In practice, however, this narrative just isn't true, and perpetuating the idea that CPS can do no wrong is only hurting families who experience legal kidnapping without cause.

It's important to note that in many cases where CPS takes custody of kids, there are no charges filed against the parents, and no arrests made. One would assume that if the abuse was bad enough to warrant removing the child from the home, then there should be criminal proceedings. Despite this, a very small minority of parents have enough evidence against them that the case holds up in court, so many legal kidnapping cases occur without formal charges of abuse or neglect. This points to a clear difference in the way these cases are viewed by CPS and by the police. The police look for evidence, and finding none, they cannot build a case. Meanwhile, CPS is able to move in without clear evidence, and can tear a family apart on information that is too flimsy to necessitate criminal charges.

The lack of arrests suggests that, in many cases, there isn't nearly enough evidence to say definitively that a child who has been removed from their home by CPS was being abused before their removal. This means many parents may have been found completely innocent if a full investigation was ever performed, but too many kids are taken without an investigation at all, and evidence to the contrary is frequently ignored. If these cases wouldn't hold up in court, it's unlikely that they would be enough to warrant a legal kidnapping, and yet this pattern of CPS overreach continues. Without accountability and a need for evidence, CPS workers are allowed to game the system for their personal gain, often with little care for the broken families they leave behind in their wake.

Medical Kidnappings

One method through which children are frequently taken from their parents unjustly is medical kidnapping. A medical kidnapping may occur when a doctor and a child's parents have a disagreement about how a medical condition should be treated. For example, your doctor may suggest a certain procedure or medication that you feel is unsafe for your child, or you may try to get your child a medication they need but face resistance from doctors. As a parent, you have a right to decide what medical care your child gets, and you also have a right to a second opinion. However, medical kidnapping cases frequently bypass these rights and take the decision out of your hands, leaving you unable to protect your child from treatments and procedures that could have long-lasting consequences for their health.

Medical kidnappings have become especially notable in the wake of COVID-19 guidelines. Government mandates that force children to wear masks and get vaccinations remove the right of the parent to make an informed decision about their child's medical care. They allow the government to dictate what is and isn't safe. They represent the government overreach that has plagued many different kinds of COVID-19 guidelines, including shutdowns and quarantines that have prevented small business owners from making enough money to support their families. These shutdowns, like mask and vaccination mandates, all represent methods by which the government attempts to dictate what you can and can't do with your life and your body. And in the case of medical kidnappings, they can have serious consequences that result in family separation if you don't know how to fight back against them. This is just another way in which children are being separated from their parents without the consent of either party, and if no one intervenes, this corruption will continue to harm families across the country.

Why Knowing Your Rights Is So Important

Currently, many lawmakers are pushing for changes that would limit the ability of Title 42 and the Adoption and Safe Families Act to encourage legal kidnappings, or repeal and replace these laws altogether. Child welfare activists are working to draw more attention to the cause, which puts additional pressure on lawmakers to correct these injustices. It is important to learn about these problems and push for change within your own community, contacting local representatives and expressing your concerns about the fact of children who are unlawfully taken by CPS and demanding change. The one thing standing in the way of this goal is that the majority of people are entirely unaware of what is happening right under their noses.

An average Joe who has never had a personal run-in with CPS isn't aware of the problems inherent in the system. In fact, most peoples' gut reaction is to defend CPS due to its reputation as a service that helps children escape dangerous situations. They are entirely unaware that there is any corruption in CPS, which means that if they ever do have to protect themselves and their kids from being separated, they don't know what they can do. They aren't aware that there are lawyers and advocates who specialize in legal kidnappings, nor do they know how to assert their rights. CPS faces little to no repercussions for these cases, even when they are in the wrong and the children are returned, because public knowledge of what CPS does wrong is not very widespread. This is a serious issue, because it means that when kids are taken from families unjustly, parents have trouble finding the support they need to win their cases. They are labeled as abusers and dismissed, when really, the problem lies with CPS's lack of accountability.

Since many people don't know how CPS is separating good families, they end up being complicit in the system. They encourage and support the actions of CPS despite not knowing the truth about them. They turn against families who are looking for help, assuming they must have done something to deserve having their kids taken away, when in reality oftentimes there is little to no evidence supporting the abuse allegations. They have been conditioned to believe that

21

CPS is a good service that protects kids, and so they don't look for fault in it, even when the evidence of corruption is readily available.

It is only through spreading the word about the problems with CPS that the corruption in CPS can be dealt with effectively. Once people learn about what is going on, they are by and large ready and willing to help. No one wants to see children suffer, after all, but if people don't recognize what's happening, there will be no public outcry, and thus no consequences for CPS workers who choose to abuse the system and profit off of laws intended to protect kids. When you learn about the dangers of letting CPS operate as it currently does and what this means for the safety of your family, you can start putting this knowledge to good use, advocating for change and spreading the word. You can also help support other families in need and push for changes, which strengthens the movement and assists families who are just trying to get their children back.

Spreading the Word

Simply spreading the word is one of the most important ways to support the movement. There is strength in numbers, as the old saying goes, and the more people who know about the problems with CPS, the easier it will be to advocate for change. This is something we discovered first-hand at a rally held in Denver, Colorado, where we spoke to the assembled crowd about what CPS is doing and how it infringes upon peoples' rights.

Many of the people in the crowd were previously unaware of any issues with CPS, or they had a very limited knowledge of the situation and they were curious to learn more. It is often hard to spread the word by traditional means, as most news outlets won't cover stories from concerned parents. We circumvented this by holding an in-person meetup and speaking to people face to face. We explained the corruption plaguing CPS to the attendees, and when they learned what was wrong, these people overwhelmingly wanted to know what they could do to help. They were willing to lend their support, but the greatest barrier that prevented them from doing so prior to the rally was that they didn't know there was anything to rally against in the first place.

Information is more important than ever these days, and how this information is distributed really matters. It is tough to trust the news, as so many stories and personal accounts are covered up. We need to reach out to people within our own communities and talk to them about what's happening, where they can learn more, and what they can do about it. This empowers us to defend ourselves against the consequences of CPS corruption and fight for lasting change.

Defending Yourself

Many people are pushing for the harmful laws that allow CPS to operate this way to change, but this takes time and collective effort. In the meantime, the best way to ensure your family is safe from the actions of CPS is to know your rights when they turn up at your door. You cannot defend yourself if you can't call out illegal and unjust actions when you see them happening. Know your rights and use them to keep your family safe.

This also means advocating for other families and helping to connect them with the right information and resources they need to fight for custody of their kids. No one in your community should have to lose their child to an unjust legal kidnapping, and it's important for parents to know that there are methods for getting their kids back which will be discussed in greater detail in future chapters.

While CPS corruption is a difficult issue for anyone to face on their own, it's important to recognize that you are not alone in your fight to keep your child safe or get them back if they have been taken by CPS. As the movement to end CPS corruption grows larger, we can all work to inspire change in our local, state, and federal governments that will ensure kids are protected from bad actors abusing the CPS and foster care system. Through collective effort, we can end unjust legal kidnappings and return children to their families.

Chapter 2

Understanding Medical Kidnapping

"It is a sad day for our country when the moral foundation of our law and the acknowledgment of God has to be hidden from public view to appease a federal judge."

Soledad O'Brien

Imagine you take your child in for their routine physical and the doctor claims to have found something concerning. You want your child to be healthy and happy, so you ask for more information, but the doctor recommends treatments you're unfamiliar with or that you've heard bad things about. Some of these treatments have side effects that could potentially be more harmful than the condition they're supposed to be fixing. As a parent, what are you supposed to do? Many parents may decide that a given medical procedure or treatment method isn't what's best for their child. Under ordinary circumstances, you should be able to seek appropriate care for your child when it is needed and ask for a second opinion before agreeing on any further steps. However, when parents and doctors disagree, this can cause CPS to step in, making your child more likely to be the victim of a medical kidnapping.

Parents have the right to decide what kind of treatment their child should receive, including preventative treatments like vaccines. You have the right to make an informed decision about your child's care. Despite this, medical kidnapping cases represent instances of CPS overreach that pressure parents to accept a particular treatment plan or risk losing their child. This might sound like something out of a horror story, but it's very real, and hundreds of families are separated by medical kidnapping each year. These cases will continue to persist until enough people provide enough resistance to change the system that allows for medical kidnapping cases, but in order to do so, you must first know what medical kidnapping is and what you can do to prevent your family from becoming victims.

What is Medical Kidnapping?

Medical kidnapping is a form of legal kidnapping that most commonly occurs inside doctor's offices and hospitals. It is a truly frightening experience for both the parents and the child, since it can result in a child being taken by CPS without sufficient evidence of abuse. Instead, medical kidnapping cases occur when medical staff perceive that a child isn't getting the right care, which is then considered neglect and grounds for CPS to intervene. While this system is in place supposedly to protect child welfare, it has become corrupted, which results in many perfectly healthy children being separated from their parents without clear cause or justification.

The most common type of medical kidnapping occurs when a doctor suggests a potentially dangerous treatment, which is then resisted by the child's parents. Many medications and procedures have serious side effects that could have long-term effects. Some doctors choose to downplay these side effects, often to the detriment of the child. For example, many common medications can have side effects ranging from pain, to dehydration, to an increased risk of seizures or psychological conditions like depression. Any parent should think carefully before considering these kinds of medications for their child. But with the threat of CPS looming over their heads, parents often feel forced to agree with

27

whatever the doctor prescribes, whether it's really the best choice for their children or not. Parents are often discouraged from seeking out a second opinion, and if they refuse the treatment, they run the risk of losing custody of their children.

Another example of a potential medical kidnapping case can be seen with the push toward forcing adults and children alike to get a COVID-19 vaccine. These vaccines are mandated by school boards more and more frequently, and some states have started requiring proof of vaccination to do basic activities like eat at a restaurant or even just to walk inside a store. These mandates take the responsibility for kids' health out of the hands of the parents, putting it into the hands of the government instead. Parents are often discouraged from doing their own research about the safety and efficacy of vaccines, with many side effects being downplayed, even when they have serious consequences for those affected. As a result, plenty of parents have taken a stand against the vaccine, worried about the adverse health effects it might cause in their children. With the threat of medical kidnapping looming over these parents, however, it will likely become more and more difficult to resist vaccine mandates for kids who could be taken by CPS. A simple desire to protect your child and to carefully consider what treatments are safe for them to get is twisted into allegations of neglect, which causes only heartbreak for the family.

In some cases, medical child abuse charges can alternatively come from treatments a parent chooses to pursue rather than ones they refused. For example, let's say you bring your child to a doctor who recommends a given treatment. You agree, but a little while later you bring your child to a different doctor, who thinks the treatment was unnecessary or that it was harmful to the child. Even though you listened to the advice of the first doctor and did what you believed was best for your child, there is still a case that the second doctor can allege that medical child abuse has occurred. They may then contact CPS and attempt to take away your child, despite the treatment's approval by a different doctor.

While medical kidnapping cases occur as a result of supposed neglect, in truth they are rarely for the benefit of the child at all, especially if there is no proof of abuse and no proper investigation performed. Instead, this is just another way that the danger of CPS rears its head, and one more way that laws meant to protect kids are exploited to endanger them.

Why Medical Kidnappings Occur

Like many other forms of CPS corruption, medical kidnapping is driven by greed and bad actors in the social services system. Thousands of people should not be losing their children when they're just trying to get treatment for a dangerous illness or preventative care, and yet this is exactly what happens every year as the problems with CPS grow worse and worse. These problems can be traced back to documents like Title 42, which encourages the separation of kids from their families under the guise of protecting public health and saving children all while rewarding the CPS employees, judges, and doctors who assist in turning over kids to the foster care system.

This corruption is further exacerbated through an abuse of power by medical professionals. All doctors must swear by the Hippocratic Oath, which is a promise to treat patients ethically and, most importantly, to "do no harm." However, when a treatment plan and its associated side effects are more dangerous to a child than foregoing the treatment altogether, is this not a violation of the Hippocratic Oath? Are these doctors not, in fact, doing harm, not just to children by forcing them to undergo potentially dangerous and experimental procedures, but also to the family unit by forcibly separating kids from their parents? You should be able to trust your health care professional, but when CPS gets involved, any parent is right to be wary about what this means for their family.

Many medical kidnapping cases also interfere with a family's freedom of religion, as guaranteed by the Bill of Rights. Plenty of modern medical procedures are unacceptable in many religions. If a proposed treatment plan goes against your faith, you should have every right to refuse it without fear of what will happen to your child if you do. Despite this, doctors frequently fail to consider religion a valid reason to forego a treatment, which leads them to claim loving parents who are acting according to their faith are supposedly committing medical child abuse.

While it is always a parents' worst nightmare for their child to be sick or injured, the threat of medical kidnapping can make this experience significantly more stressful, and can have long-lasting effects on your child's health and their overall well-being. Still, there are ways for you to defend yourself if you are a victim of medical kidnapping, or if you suspect you may become a victim of medical kidnapping. As always, the fight for custody of your kids begins with arming yourself with knowledge of your inalienable rights and liberties under the law.

Know Your Medical Rights

Federal and state laws contain many provisions to protect patients of all ages when they have a disagreement with their doctors. All patients should be able to decide which treatments and procedures are acceptable and which are not, or if they are minors, to place this decision into the hands of their parents or guardians. In many cases of medical

31

kidnapping, the actions of CPS violate these laws, as they interfere with your rights to remain in control of your child's care and to prevent medical malpractice. Despite this, most parents and even many lawyers who argue on their behalf don't know about the protections in place to prevent medical kidnappings, and so children end up separated from their families. If you ever find yourself in the middle of a medical kidnapping case, it is crucial to familiarize yourself with the relevant laws so you can defend your family.

CPS, alongside doctors and other medical care providers, can interfere with your ability to determine the type of care your child receives, as well as to question the safety and efficacy of any treatment. These situations are illegal because they violate rights granted to you by legislators and previous Supreme Court cases. Your best defense against these injustices is to be able to cite specific laws in favor of your case, which you can then reference in any potential court cases or **affidavits.**

Making Decisions About Your Child's Care

Despite what corrupt CPS workers may believe, the law as it stands does not support children being taken from their families without parental consent, nor does it encourage healthcare workers to disregard the will of childrens' parents when discussing and administering treatments. The law is meant to protect kids from abuse and neglect, and even though it has been twisted to allow for increased rates of family separation through medical kidnapping, the fact of the matter is that this practice doesn't have much legal precedent. In fact, the exact opposite is true, as the law actually affirms the role of the parent or guardian in their child's healthcare.

To see just how seriously your right to choose your child's medical care is taken, you need look no further than the case of Troxel v. Granville, 530 U.S. 57. This case, which took place in the year 2000, affirmed parental rights in healthcare settings in the face of medical overreach, as well as restricting visitation rights by parties other than the parents. It centered around a dispute over a Washington code that allowed for "'[a]ny person' to petition for visitation rights 'at any time' and authorizes state superior courts to grant such rights whenever visitation may serve a child's best interest." The case made its way all the way up to the U.S. Supreme Court, who ruled against the law and in favor of a parent's right to limit others' access to their child. In particular, the case's primary holding reaffirmed the "fundamental right under the Fourteenth Amendment for a parent to oversee the care, custody, and control of a child," (Justia, n.d., para. 1 & 6) meaning that other parties are not allowed to interfere with your basic right to raise your child as you see fit as long as your child isn't being abused. The ability of third parties to petition the courts for visitation rights, superseding the will of the parents, was ruled as unconstitutional.

What does this mean for medical kidnapping cases? For one, it means you have every right to restrict access to your child, even from doctors and other healthcare professionals. If you no longer want your child to see a certain doctor and you want to seek out a second opinion, or if you want to take your child out of a treatment you believe is causing them harm, you have the right to do so as a parent. As of the Troxel v. Granville ruling, parents' wishes are given more significant weight, and it takes a serious issue that can be proven through hard evidence of abuse or neglect to override them. Of course, even though this protection is in place, it isn't exactly common knowledge. This means that many parents who could benefit from it don't even know it exists, which empowers CPS to continue taking kids without any pushback. When you know and assert your parental rights, you have a much better chance of making a case for yourself and preventing the state from taking your child.

Note that as a parent, you have the right to refuse any medical treatment you think may be dangerous to your child. You have the authority to make medical decisions that are in your child's best interests. While healthcare professionals can challenge these decisions if they have a difference of opinion, if you are not harming your child and you simply want to pursue a different treatment method, no doctor is guaranteed access to your child to perform procedures that you have not approved. Only you know what's best for your child, which is why the law protects your ability to make decisions about their medical care.

Questioning Suggested Treatments

Not every treatment is a perfect fit for every patient, even if the illness is the same. For example, an otherwise healthy adult who gets cancer would likely be benefitted by chemotherapy or radiation therapy treatments. It would likely be in their best interests to agree to these treatments once they felt fully informed and confident about their decision to undergo them, with all relevant knowledge of their side effects. On the other hand, asking a kid to go through the same treatments might not be a choice that is beneficial to the child. Treatments like chemotherapy take their toll on the body, and this toll is amplified in young children who shouldn't have to experience the side effects of either cancer or some of its more aggressive treatment methods.

Of course, not every trip to the hospital or doctor's office involves such a serious diagnosis, but the point remains the same: a given treatment may be better suited to one individual or situation over another. CPS would have you believe that the person who gets to make the call about whether a given treatment is right for your child is their doctor, but in reality, it is you, the parent or guardian. If you are uncomfortable proceeding with a treatment until you feel like you fully understand all the risks, or if you feel that the risks outweigh the benefits, you can choose to pursue an alternate treatment method. You also have the right to ask for more information about a given treatment before you approve or reject it, which allows you to make a more informed decision. While the medical expertise of doctors and specialists is often invaluable, parents should be part of the treatment process too, so be sure to speak up if you have questions about whether a given treatment is safe or necessary. You should never be made to feel too intimidated to voice your concerns, as this violates your rights as a parent.

Any child who is under the age of 18 is legally considered a minor, and thus as a parent you have full access to their health records. A doctor should never attempt to keep records private from you, nor should they withhold information about your child's treatment. Be sure to request official records of all recommended treatments as well as any treatments your child receives, and copies of their charts and relevant documents too. This serves a dual purpose. It will help you stay informed about your child's care, and it will also give you evidence of the timeline of events if you ever have to bring a medical kidnapping case to court.

You should also be cautious about which doctors you allow to make recommendations about your child's health. Not all doctors are equally skilled, and many have different methods for treating the same illness. If you take your child to a specialist, be sure to research their qualifications so you know if your child is getting the best possible care. If you are uncertain about a particular diagnosis or proposed procedure, you and your child have the right to see a different doctor to get a second opinion before you proceed with any kind of treatment. Sometimes, you may need to see multiple doctors before you find one who aligns with your family values, respects your opinions as a parent, and truly wants to help your child. The threat of medical kidnapping should never be a barrier between sick children and the help they need, so assert your right to a second opinion if you feel like you aren't getting the best possible care from their current doctor.

While laws like Title 42 pit the government against parents and facilitate legal kidnappings, the law as a whole overwhelmingly supports the right of parents to make appropriate medical decisions for their children. If CPS takes legal action against you, seek out a lawyer who is well-versed in medical kidnapping cases who can help you navigate this difficult experience, but at the same time, don't sell your own powers as a parent short. Remember your rights so you can protect your child's welfare against instances of state overreach.

Sharing Your Resources With Impacted Families

If you haven't been the victim of a medical kidnapping case yourself, there's still a chance you may know another family who is experiencing the painful loss of a child thanks to corruption in the medical field and within CPS. It might feel like there is little you can do to help since you aren't directly related to the case, but now that you know why medical kidnapping occurs and how it is frequently performed under unlawful pretenses, you can assist these families. The primary ways to do so are through sharing your knowledge and connecting other families with the resources they need to fight back against CPS and reclaim their kids.

You already have a good understanding of the laws that protect parents from having their children taken away under medical kidnapping cases. Work as an advocate in your community to share this information. Just letting distraught parents know there's something they can do to help get their children back can give them hope during one of the most difficult times of their lives, which makes all the difference. Sharing your knowledge also ensures they are better prepared to assert their rights when fighting back against CPS, which benefits all parents. The more pushback CPS gets when they attempt to subvert the rights of parents, the more difficult it will be for them to take more kids in the future, and the greater the likelihood that legislators will catch wind of the corruption and work to outlaw it.

Don't forget to make use of all the resources available to you and other parents. Seek legal counsel when you need it. Refer back to legislative documents, all of which are publically available. Know your rights, and work with local experts like David Jose who will help you affirm these rights in the face of injustice. By spreading the word, you are enabling more parents to fight back against CPS overreach in all its forms, and helping to put an end to unjustified medical kidnapping cases once and for all.

Chapter 3

The Importance of Education

"The courts and the media elite] are abolishing America, they are deconstructing our country...they have dethroned our God."

Pat Buchanan

If you come away from this book knowing just one thing more than you did when you first sat down with it, make it this: knowledge is power, and without taking the steps to educate yourself, you don't know what you don't know. People, organizations, and yes, even the government, will lie and take advantage of you if you don't know any better. If you aren't sure how to defend yourself, you are only putting yourself at a disadvantage. Make no mistake; this is exactly what agencies like CPS want.

Now more than ever before, the right to education held by all Americans is in jeopardy. School boards work to remove inconvenient information from the curriculum. They refuse to teach certain topics deemed controversial or labeled as harmful, even when they're important aspects of families' lives. Religious expression is frequently suppressed, and perhaps most importantly of all, people across the nation are no longer being taught about the Constitution and their rights under the law.

What's the purpose of all of this suppression of information? Why do educators consistently push for American students to improve their grades, but fail to give kids the tools they need to succeed? Many have argued that these kinds of changes in the curriculum are purposeful attempts to prevent the general populace from standing up for their rights. After all, you cannot defend yourself with a law or a part of the Constitution if you don't know it exists, or that it applies to your situation. By refusing to teach students basic information about their rights, schools allow bad actors like CPS to walk all over the American populace without any form of recourse. This needs to end, and the best way to do it is through education.

The Most Effective Way to Fight Back Against Corruption

Protecting children is a goal that any good person can get behind. Despite this, you don't see many protests in the street supporting the cause of ending CPS corruption. Why is this? If there is a clear issue with the way CPS is currently being run, why don't more people want to fix it, and why isn't anything being done about the issue? The main roadblock preventing CPS reform currently is a lack of knowledge about the situation from the general public.

You're sure to pick up on this lack of knowledge if you try speaking to your friends and family members about the problems with CPS. If they only follow the mainstream news or they're not very into politics and activism, they will likely have no idea what you're talking about. They might be confused, surprised, or skeptical that these terrible things could be happening in their own country, and often within their own state. Worse, they might try to argue in support of CPS, unknowingly defending people who put children in greater danger because they have been taught to see CPS as infallible heroes. In short, your average person is completely uneducated about the situation. They take their cues from what government agencies and their supporters tell them, and they don't know there's any reason to look into the issue further, at least not until they find themselves in a situation where they are pitted against CPS.

When people are uneducated about the big issues, important causes stagnate. If no one cares, there is little reason for lawmakers and other people in positions of power to care and to listen to advocates asking for change. There are few if any people demanding they do something about this issue, so they choose to do nothing. Meanwhile, the general public doesn't know there's anything wrong in the first place. Those who do know, through personal experience or otherwise, may still be uncertain about if there's anything they can do to support the cause or to fight CPS for custody of their kids. When the masses remain blind to the issues at hand, nothing is done to keep organizations like CPS in check.

On the other hand, when people learn about everything that's wrong with the current system, they're often more than willing to get involved. Every time we have held a public rally to talk about CPS corruption, good people have attended, listened, learned, and then asked what they can do to help. When peoples' eyes are opened to the truths of the world, they become allies to the cause, and they increase the power of the people. Vocal activists and figureheads are all well and good, but they accomplish very little without a base of supporters. The more people who care about a cause, the more voices that join the chant for things to change, and the more the movement builds momentum. In other words, education gives the power back to the people, where it belongs.

There's a reason why so few people know about the dangers of CPS, and to discover it, you only need to ask yourself who would be best served by covering up this information. Many people in government roles who benefit from the current state of laws like Title 42 have a vested interest in keeping these laws on the books. This includes CPS employees who profit from taking kids out of their homes, bad foster parents who take a check and neglect the kids in their care, those complicit in child trafficking and the disappearances of hundreds of kids who enter the foster care system every year, and other government employees who receive part of the payout from CPS cases, such as corrupt judges. These influences make their way to the media and work to suppress news stories that would otherwise provide a window into the experiences of families who have been torn apart because of CPS meddling. The experiences of real kids and parents who have to live with the aftermath of legal kidnappings are brushed under the rug, all to keep people out of the loop so they will remain complacent with the current system.

It is no surprise that this lack of education also extends to depriving parents of the tools they could otherwise use to get their children back once CPS gets involved. Many parents feel hopeless when CPS comes knocking because no one has ever told them how to argue their case. They see that the vast majority of people who have their kids taken by CPS don't get them back, and worse, that parents lose all contact with their children and all knowledge of their whereabouts. They see attorneys who are supposedly well-versed in CPS cases trying and failing to get kids returned, in part because they are working within the system designed to make them fail. They're worried about what will happen to their kids, but they don't know what to do about it, all because they haven't been properly educated about their rights. The less any parent knows about CPS and the laws governing it, the harder it is to prevent them from taking kids. It is only through spreading the word and educating people that the outcome of these custody cases will start to change. With enough momentum, the laws themselves may even change, enabling more oversight of CPS and stamping out the corruption that takes its toll on families every day. Educate yourself and others around you, because knowledge is power.

People In Power Fear the Educated

In the Medieval days of kings and feudalism, the general population was uneducated. Most children didn't attend school, and grew up only learning how to work on their parents' farms. Many did not know how to do basic math, and many more could not read or write at all. This wasn't just a fluke though. After all, the noble children were receiving an education. They had access to schooling and other resources, all so they could better learn how to control the uneducated masses. Knowledge was withheld from the people who worked in the fields, because the people in power knew that if they could suppress education, they could create a group of people who didn't think to question why they had no rights, and who didn't know enough to be dissatisfied with living a life of slavery.

In the modern day, most American children have access to public schooling. The average child can read and write. Still, there are gaps in their education, and these gaps are just as purposeful as they were in Medieval times. Kids grow up to be adults who remain blissfully unaware of what they don't know, and the cycle perpetuates itself, all in favor of those at the top of the hierarchy. A lack of knowledge means a lack of political power, and this is just how those currently in power want to keep things.

The fact of the matter is, anyone in power wants to hold onto that power, and the best way to do so is to keep everyone else uneducated. Let's say a parent gets their child taken away by CPS in a way that isn't permitted by the law. CPS benefits if they can keep the child away from their family, even though they subverted the law to do so. If the parent knows their rights, they can argue their case with a good chance of having their child returned to them. If they don't, they won't know what to say and which laws to point to if they want to prove that CPS was out of line, which means they are less likely to be successful. CPS and everyone else benefiting from legal kidnapping cases has a clear interest in ensuring as few people know the laws protecting their rights as possible, and this is reflected in the ways people are taught about the law, specifically about how difficult it is to study legal documents.

Read the Law Yourself

If someone asked you to read through your state's constitution right now, what would you say? Would you get right to work looking through the document? Or, more likely, would you avoid the task because it is too hard? After all, there's all that legal jargon that a layperson wouldn't understand. You'd likely need to hire a lawyer who is well-versed in the state constitution to explain it to you if you wanted to have any hope of learning what it says, right? This is what most people assume, but in reality, it just isn't true. In fact, many legal documents are far less complex than you may have been led to believe, and are instead written in plain English that the average Joe could understand.

When you actually look at the text of documents like state constitutions, you see that they're not so difficult to understand after all. Take, for example, the Arizona constitution. Under the Declaration of Rights, your rights as a citizen are stated clearly with few to no complicated terms. You'll find simple descriptions such as "No person shall be deprived of life, liberty, or property without due process of law" and, "The right of petition, and of the people peaceably to assemble for the common good, shall never be abridged" (Arizona Const. art. II, pt. 4 & 6). While there might be an unfamiliar term or two, the law is surprisingly readable because it is important for every citizen to know their rights. If you want to know every right you have that is protected by the federal and state constitutions, the average person is capable of reading these documents themselves with little issue.

Despite this, the vast majority of people believe that all legal documents are difficult to read, even when being able to read these documents is key to understanding your rights. If state constitutions are so easy to read after all, why is there this misunderstanding? One explanation is that the more people believe they won't understand the constitution, the less likely they are to attempt to read it. This means fewer people know their rights, and the average person doesn't know how to defend themselves against CPS and other violations of their constitutional rights.

If you want to equip yourself with knowledge to prevent anyone from taking advantage of you, the biggest leg-up you can give yourself is to read the law. In many cases, you'll find that organizations like CPS are banking on you having no knowledge of your state constitution, which they may violate when taking custody of a child. You don't need to be a lawyer to read about your rights; you don't even have to have gone to college. Of course, this common perception of the law as something difficult or impossible for most people to understand isn't a mistake. It only serves to reinforce a lack of education that begins all the way back in grade school.

School Sabotage

Between mask mandates and concerns over school curriculum, the topic of what is being taught in schools is an especially important one these days. Teachers and school boards have a responsibility to teach your kids everything they need to know and to leave harmful ideas that are inappropriate for school out of the classroom. You trust your child's school system to educate them, but in many cases, they may not be so deserving of your trust. Many concerned parents have pointed out that in recent years, it seems like key topics are disappearing from the curriculum left and right. Kids are missing out on important life lessons, and good family values have all but vanished from classrooms. One of the most important things many education plans gloss over nowadays is the constitution, and this has serious effects on how well-informed people are about their rights.

Civics isn't taking center stage in history curriculums like it used to. A recent study of high schoolers in Oklahoma found that out of 1000 kids surveyed, "only 3% would be able to pass the U.S. Immigration Services' citizenship exam," and a similar study in Arizona also found that "only 3.5% of public high school students would be able to pass the citizenship test" (Whitehead, 2011, para. 2-3). This lack of knowledge points to serious flaws in the way kids are educated today. The majority of kids are constitutionally illiterate, and these kids grow up to become adults who don't know the first thing about the Bill or Rights or any other legal documents protecting their freedoms. As a result, they don't know when the government's actions threaten their civil liberties, and they also don't know how to argue against unlawful acts. This problem can only be remedied through educating yourself, your children, and your neighbors. When everyone knows their rights, they will be able to recognize violations of these rights for what they are, and stand together to stop them.

How Education Leads to Change

When it comes to enacting change, nothing is more powerful than having an educated group of people all working together to achieve the same goal. One or two voices calling for change aren't very powerful. Even the most educated people have trouble standing against corrupt systems on their own, especially when these systems are as powerful as government bodies. However, when people band together and demand change, even on a local or community level, everyone in the group has more power. It is this collective action that has shaped America's history, from its very beginnings during the Revolutionary War all the way through to the modern day. Wherever there is corruption, there are good people willing to stand against it, as long as they are made aware of the problem.

If you want to fight back against CPS corruption, start in your own community. Talk to your friends and family about the issues with CPS, since many people are entirely unaware. Reach out to parents who are struggling to get their children back and provide them with the resources they need to win their battle. As you'll see in the following chapters, you don't need to be a lawyer to help return kids to their families so long as you know your rights and you can mobilize your community, just like David did. The more you learn about how David helped to return dozens of kids to their families, the better you will understand what strategies are most effective and how you can employ them if you ever find yourself up against CPS.

Chapter 4

Bringing Kids Home

"The destiny of every country is in the hands of the people who know God."

Sunday Adelaja

One day, David was walking out of the CPS courthouse when he noticed a Hispanic woman outside who was obviously distressed. The woman was crying and repeating, "I can't see my babies." At the time, David was just at the beginning of his own fight to get his kids back, who had been taken by CPS as well. He knew he and the woman shared common ground, and he wanted to reach out to someone in the same position he was in. When David's kids were taken, all he wanted was for someone to reassure him that it would be okay and he would get to see him again, so he and his wife did exactly that for the distraught woman. Of course, she was far from the only parent there experiencing the heartbreak of losing a child. Just a few steps away there was a white woman in the same situation, and thousands of other parents have found themselves in the same spot over the years. No matter what someone's culture, race, or age may be, having a child taken away is devastating. It can feel impossible to fight back in these situations, but sometimes all you need is someone reassuring you that they've been where you are, and that things are going to be okay.

At that moment, David realized he had a decision to make. He could continue to play the game the courts were goading him into, following their rules and trying only to get his own kids back while other parents in his same position had little hope of doing the same. Or he could stand up to the corruption of CPS and fight for all families who had their kids legally kidnapped under false and unfair pretenses. When presented with this decision, the choice was obvious: David had to do the right thing.

Many parents despair that they will never be able to get their children returned from CPS. Unfortunately, the vast majority of lawyers who are meant to help people regain custody of their kids consistently fail to do so. These attorneys might return one or two kids a year out of the dozens of cases they take on. They may not do this on purpose, but lawyers who play by the rules they were taught in law school, without becoming experts in Constitutional law and without questioning whether the current system is fair for parents, just don't know how to properly declare their rights and convince the courts their clients should have their children returned. As a result, parents think even the best help money can buy is failing them, and they have very little faith that they will get to see their kids again. Without hope, no one challenges CPS and the courts, and the corruption goes unchecked. However, David knew that if he could peel back the wallpaper and expose all of the flaws of CPS, he could restore parents' lost hope. Even when he was threatened with jail time for exposing the truth about CPS, he pushed onward with his plan to educate people, all in service of helping them get their kids back.

David's plan was a simple one, founded on the idea that knowledge is one of the strongest weapons anyone can wield. First, he studied the law, getting familiar enough with it that he could go toe-to-toe with anyone looking to challenge him. He also studied the Bible, because he knew that the journey he was about to take was a mission from God to help people in need. Then, he shared what he had learned with others. Bible passages provided people with the faith, strength, and hope they needed to keep pushing forward during one of the most difficult periods of their lives. The law provided them with the tools they needed to convince the courts that CPS had unjustly taken their kids. These two texts, when taken together, proved to be a powerful force, and allowed David to help over 90 families who had been unconstitutionally separated from their kids.

Success Stories

By choosing to do the right thing, David's work has had a significant impact on parents who would have otherwise lacked the tools and knowledge necessary to get their kids back. David knew he had to get information out to the public about the problems with CPS and the courts, and to do so, he would need to work to reach as large of an audience as possible. He started creating videos that detailed all of the problems laws like Title 42 have caused, as well as informing parents about what they can do about them, on his YouTube channel. These videos provided a lifeline to struggling parents, helping to educate the people so they could fight back against CPS.

In 2018, David worked with ex-military intelligence agent David Straight to create an informative video teaching people about the law and how it could be used to protect their families. Over the course of the video, they explained the child trafficking scandal allegations behind CPS and exposed other forms of corruption in the courts. The video received tens of thousands of views, and it also attracted the attention of CPS and the courts, who didn't want this information being spread to the public. However, the damage was already done. People were already learning that by sending in **affidavits** and working together with other parents who had been through similar circumstances, they could successfully make their case for their children to be returned to their loving home.

Putting out these videos changed the tides in favor of the parents. Woken up to what was happening right under their nose, parents and concerned citizens across the country learned about the movement and wanted to support it. They put pressure on CPS to follow the law and stop unjust seizures of children, and to return kids who had been illegally taken from their homes. During this time, many families were able to get their kids back, including one woman who had the same judge and attorney who had presided over David's own case. Because the woman had watched the videos and informed herself, she knew to call out court procedures that violated her rights, and she demanded her kids back. She had the confidence and skill set she needed, and it paid off: all nine of her kids were returned to her custody. To show their thanks, they even sent David a postcard of the family together again, tie-dying shirts, and gave him a plate at the next Thanksgiving.

In another, similar case, David assisted with sending out **affidavits** after a woman was under attack by the courts after seizing her kids. They insisted she was an unfit mother and she would never get her kids back. Through the power of affidavits and putting the woman's new knowledge of CPS and the law to good use, she and David proved them wrong. Four kids returned to the home, where they still live to this day, over two years later. Other families benefited from consent agreements, where courts agreed to return children to their homes in exchange for not being sued over all the CPS corruption the parents had experienced first-hand. In one such situation, not only was the case dropped and the kids returned, but also the prosecutor assigned to the case was tried criminally.

In each of these cases, every family had one trick up their sleeve: knowledge. As the Bible says, **"Woe unto you, lawyers! for ye have taken away the key of knowledge"** (King James Bible, Luke 11:52). Fighting CPS is all about giving this key of knowledge back to the people. If the first mother had never watched David's videos, she wouldn't have known that there was hope for her to reunite with her kids. If the next mother hadn't known about the power of affidavits, she might not have been able to use them to her advantage to get her kids back. If families across the nation remained unaware of the corruption of CPS and how their actions violated their rights as parents, no consent agreements would have been struck. In short, the better informed people are about the law, their rights, and what's going on in the world around them, the better their chances are of recognizing injustice when it occurs, and the more hope they will have to restore their families. For families looking to repair the damage and get their kids back, the first step to take is to better understand what an affidavit is and how it can be used to help fight corruption.

Understanding Affidavits

If you are ever brought into a courtroom to give your testimony, you will need to swear under oath that you are not lying to the court. You may have heard the question "do you swear to tell the truth, the whole truth, and nothing but the truth?" on legal dramas and other TV shows. Anyone giving testimony in a court of law must tell the truth to the best of their knowledge, as lying is considered to be perjury, a felony that can potentially result in fines and jail time. In some cases, however, there may be a need to collect someone's testimony outside of the courtroom. When you need to give sworn testimony outside of a courtroom setting, you may be asked to sign an **affidavit**, which serves a similar purpose.

When you make a statement and sign an **affidavit,** you are claiming that what you have said is entirely factual, and you are putting your statement on the record officially. Once it has been signed by a notary public or another official with the authority to administer an oath, it can then be used in future legal proceedings if necessary. Any time you sign an affidavit, you should make sure everything on the document is true, as it could spell future legal trouble if you lie. However, when used correctly, affidavits can be incredibly powerful, especially when it comes to dealing with CPS.

Let's say that CPS comes to your doorstep to perform a home visit, but while they are there, they do something that violates your constitutional rights. For example, they may attempt to proceed with an investigation or try to take your child without your consent, even though there is no clear and immediate threat of danger to your child that would normally be required to bypass parental consent. Since you have witnessed this, you can write an affidavit with your testimony that can then be used to inform people about what has occurred and why it's a violation of your rights. Even better, affidavits give law enforcement the ability to take the case to court and charge the CPS employees who violated your rights. The more of these cases that get taken to court, the harder it will be for CPS to hide accusations of corruption, and the more investigations will be launched into CPS for their conduct.

Affidavits are even more powerful when multiple people send them for the same issue. Having testimony from many different sources helps to reduce the doubt that might otherwise turn these cases into "he said, she said." When hundreds or even thousands of people have seen CPS corruption for themselves and they are willing to testify to it, courts are forced to take the concerns of parents and community members seriously, which helps to root out corruption. In other words, affidavits ensure people who violate parents' rights will face consequences for their actions. Affidavits have two main benefits that make them especially useful tools in the fight against CPS. They result in greater transparency from CPS and other government organizations, and they also allow the people to feel empowered.

Transparency

Ordinarily, if you have a complaint about how you have been treated by the court or by CPS, your attorney might suggest that you file a bar or judicial complaint, known as a grievance. Attorneys and judges with grievances filed against them are subject to more intense scrutiny and review, and they run the risk of having their license to practice taken away due to misconduct, or at least this is how things play out in theory. In practice, however, these complaints often end up being as worthless as a blank page. They are frequently ignored, thrown out, or overlooked, and they're rarely passed on to anyone who is willing to take a stand against corrupt judges and attorneys. Many cases get blocked from ever even reaching the court, let alone the bar association, because attorneys protect their own. It's a classic case of the fox guarding the hen house to ensure that CPS can continue to operate without fear of backlash.

When you sign an affidavit, you are putting your testimony on the record in a way that cannot be so easily ignored. You are working to get the word out about corruption and the underhanded actions taken by CPS employees in an effort to separate as many families as possible. Affidavits from hundreds of families helped David notify the Arizona Supreme Court that these illegal and unconstitutional actions were happening within their jurisdiction, and this amount of transparency wouldn't have been possible without people who were willing to lend their voice and testimony to the cause. Additionally, affidavits prevent government officials from lying and trying to sweep these claims under the rug with their own testimony, because they don't want to run the risk of committing perjury. By surpassing the smaller courts and going right to the legislators who have the power to directly impact the law, both the legislators and the people can stay informed about corruption without interference.

Empowerment

Greater transparency translates directly into greater empowerment. If you are just one person fighting against CPS, or trying to convince the state Supreme Court to change the laws, you're going to have a tough time getting anyone to listen to you. If you're the only one who has submitted a grievance against a corrupt attorney or judge, you'll likely experience the same roadblocks. Your concerns will be easier to ignore and brush aside because you are on your own. However, through the power of affidavits, you don't have to tackle these challenges alone. Many people lend their voices to the fight, which leads to greater coverage and helps to spread the word to even more people. The movement grows and grows, and with each new supporter, the group's power to enact real change grows as well.

Affidavits demonstrate that regular people have political power when they work together. They prove that you don't need a law degree to understand your rights, and you don't need to be elected to any official government position to make a difference in your community. They empower people to take a stand, and they are the secret to success for Josh and David's efforts to always work with the people and do the right thing.

Why David Succeeds

Since David got involved as an advocate, he has seen much greater rates of success with getting kids returned to their parents than many attorneys have. Even those who claim to specialize in CPS cases often struggle to win their cases, and yet through affidavits and a grassroots movement,

David has managed to return over 90 kids, with more on the way. Many critics might wonder how it is possible that someone with no formal training, who is entirely self-taught regarding the law, could have much more success than those who paid thousands of dollars in law school tuition and who had to pass the bar, getting so many qualifications that ultimately do little to help them win their cases. Contrary to what they may believe, it is exactly David's status as an outsider to the system that enables him to succeed where others have failed.

Attorneys who get all of their training from law school and internships only know how to work within the system and follow the guidelines that others have laid out for them. They want to make friends, and they don't want to do anything that would risk getting them blacklisted or hurting their careers. They may also be ignorant of the laws of the state Constitution because they are relying on other peoples' interpretations of these laws, rather than taking the time to learn and study them for themselves. Because of this, these attorneys often don't realize that CPS has violated their clients' rights, so they do not take the opportunity to point this out. Even when they do recognize that a violation has occurred, they might submit a grievance or otherwise try to work out the issue through the courts, which is unlikely to work because everyone in the system protects each other.

Meanwhile, David approaches situations as an outsider, but one who has taken the time to really get to know the laws he is citing. He knows what it takes to expose corruption, and he knows how to utilize affidavits to his advantage to help families get their kids back. Anyone who has studied laws for as long as David has can walk into these situations with confidence, because they know the law is on their side, and they only have to read the law to prove it. State Constitutions are not difficult to understand, and it is this simplicity that helps give power back to the everyman. The truth is that no one needs a special license to understand the law and use it to their advantage. The founding fathers themselves didn't need approval or licenses from any outside organization to write the Constitution. The idea that you need years of education to dip your toes into the legal world is simply untrue, and David's work exemplifies this fact, reinforcing the power of the people through affidavits.

It's easy to see the powerful effect affidavits have had in combating CPS corruption. What some don't realize is that this power is available to all citizens. Of the 2,000 affidavits David collected and sent to President Trump's Advisory Council on Human Trafficking to notify them of the issues with CPS, many were gathered from regular concerned parents, often people who were coached through the process via Facebook. No one involved was considered an expert by typical standards, and yet when they mobilized together, they were able to enact real change that saved many children's lives.

Taking a Stand Against Human Trafficking

Ideally, any child who is taken from a home deemed to be dangerous by CPS should at least be placed in a new home that is safe and takes care of them. However, when looking at the realities of the foster care system, it isn't hard to see how this assumption starts to break down. It's no big secret that foster care can be a dangerous place for kids. Many children who have grown up in foster families or in halfway houses have come out of them with horror stories of abuse, neglect, and other forms of mistreatment. Others disappear into the system entirely, after CPS supposedly "loses track" of them, with no guarantees of their safety. If CPS really cares about the wellbeing of the kids they take, there should be clear records of where each child ends up alongside frequent check-ins to ensure their new home is really a safe one. Instead, rather than providing many of these kids with better lives, the actions of CPS often only fuel the human trafficking industry, putting kids in real danger.

When you think of the term human trafficking, your mind likely goes to cases of sex trafficking, but in truth the definition is much more broad than that. Trafficking refers to any instance of taking a minor from one jurisdiction, or state, to another without the consent of their parents. In this way, it's easy to see how CPS feeds into the human trafficking industry, as their main purpose is to relocate kids. They don't get parental permission to rehome the vast majority of the kids they take, even though this is illegal. Of course, trafficking is often more insidious than this definition suggests, and many kids end up as victims. Once kids who have been taken by CPS are placed in new homes, these homes often aren't properly monitored to ensure kids are safe. Once kids are separated from their parents, they are vulnerable to trafficking.

In fact, one report from Reuters indicates that "one in seven children reported missing was likely a victim of sex trafficking and of those, 88 percent were in the care of child welfare when they went missing" (Wulfhorst, 2018, para. 20). Kids in foster homes are often under a less careful watch than kids who are allowed to stay with their families, and their sense of trust with authority figures may be fractured. This provides opportunities for traffickers to take kids, at which point they disappear from the CPS database.

While some CPS employees undoubtedly have good intentions, the facts are clear: kids in the child welfare system are at a much greater risk of ending up in child trafficking. This is no mere coincidence. Therefore, fighting to bring kids home who have been taken by CPS isn't just about reuniting families. It's also about protecting kids and fighting against human trafficking.

Hiding in Plain Sight

One especially common misconception about child trafficking is that traffickers are "no names." If you watch movies like Taken and similar films, the people engaging in trafficking aren't well-known public figures. They are shady men who aim to stay out of the limelight so they can avoid scrutiny. In real life, however, this often isn't the case. Instead, many people involved in human trafficking are actually some of the biggest names in the country, even those who have close ties to notable traffickers like Jeffrey Epstein.

In July of 2019, Jeffrey Epstein was arrested on charges of sex trafficking. In January of 2020, the public was shocked to learn that these charges weren't unknown prior to Epstein's arrest. In fact, many people considered Epstein's connection to child trafficking to be an open secret, and were thus complicit in the continued endangerment of kids. The admission came from Cindy McCain, John McCain's widow, who revealed that she and many others were aware of what Epstein was doing, and yet they did not bring this to public attention. In a recording from the State of the World 2020 conference in Florida, McCain admits, "Epstein was hiding in plain sight. We all knew about him. We all knew what he was doing, but we had [...] no legal aspect that would go after him. They were afraid of him" (C-SPAN, 2020). It is almost unbelievable to hear that someone as well-known as McCain turned a blind eye to a known child trafficker, and yet it is the truth by her own testimony. It further showcases how many big-name figures may claim to be advocates for children publicly, but who fail to inform the public about the serious child trafficking offenses going on right under their noses. Another case of notable public figures getting caught up in child trafficking cases comes in the form of the story of Laura Silsby and the New Life Children's Refuge.

The New Life Children's Refuge

In the wake of the Haiti earthquake in 2010, many U.S. missionaries wanted to provide support for those affected by the natural disaster. However, not everyone was there to help. One such missionary was Laura Silsby. She, along with nine accomplices, were caught attempting to cross the border out of Haiti and into the Dominican Republic while also transporting 33 Haitian kids. The group claimed they were trying to bring the kids to safety, but Haitian officials believed they had ulterior motives and brought them up on charges of human trafficking. While eventually these charges were dropped for her accomplices, Silsby remained in jail in Haiti because she was the founder of the New Life Children's Refuge (NLCR), and thus was responsible for the organization's actions.

Despite what their defense claimed, what the NLCR was doing was very much illegal. They were bringing kids across country lines without parental consent, potentially to separate them from their families permanently. NLCR members insisted that the children were orphans, but further investigation revealed that the majority of the kids still had living parents. As a result, the charges stuck, and Silsby found herself in hot water. Even her legal representation reflected further corruption, as her attorney, Jorge Puello, was also battling sex trafficking charges of his own from El Salvador. He faced further legal trouble, and even while serving as Silsby's lawyer, he was "wanted by the police in at least four countries in connection with charges including sex trafficking of girls and women, and making counterfeit documents and violating parole" (Lacey & Urbina, 2010, para. 3). Eventually, Silsby was able to argue her charges down to "arranging irregular travel," for which she was found guilty and served jail time.

Unfortunately, Silsby's tale of corruption doesn't end there. One might assume that a woman convicted of a crime related to a child trafficking attempt would have no place in the U.S. CPS system. However, in truth, Silsby received a pardon from then-president Bill Clinton. Worse, she later began working at AlertSense, a company responsible for sending out amber alerts and which handles many reports of potential child trafficking cases. The very same company that should have been standing in opposition to people like Silsby was, in fact, employing her.

If Silsby's story proves anything, it is that the corruption in CPS runs deeper than most of the public would ever imagine. The idea that someone who was charged with a very notable child trafficking case would find herself working for AlertSense a mere few years later, and that she would have support from big political figures like Bill and Hillary Clinton, is almost unthinkable. However, once you know the truth about CPS, it is easy to see how known attempted child traffickers can easily infiltrate the system. This is why it is so important to David and others like him who are fighting the good fight to bring kids home. Once kids are taken by CPS, parents don't have any control over where they go or what happens to them. It is only by exposing the corruption and returning kids to their parents that families can have true peace of mind. Additionally, the more these cases are spoken about and the more the public is informed, the easier it will be to utilize collective action to fight for real change, not just for individual families but on the state and federal level.

Chapter 5

Working Toward Legislative Change

"It can not be emphasized too strongly or too often that this great nation was founded, not by religionists, but by Christians, not on religions, but on the gospel of Jesus Christ."

Anonymous

Returning kids to their families is an important task, but it's even more important to ensure kids aren't able to be taken from their families in the first place. Parents should not have to live in fear that CPS will turn up, make false claims about them based on little to no evidence, insult their parenting abilities, and take away their kids without their consent. Likewise, kids should not have to live their lives worried that they will be separated from their parents. This can have a serious psychological impact on the whole family, putting a lot of stress on the parents and potentially traumatizing the kids who are pulled away from their homes and sometimes their cultures to be placed with a family who doesn't know or understand them like their own parents do.

To prevent this, it's imperative to work toward changing the legislature that encourages CPS to unconstitutionally take kids and rewards them for doing so. Laws like Title 42 cannot be allowed to stand. At the same time, these laws are much harder to fight than individual cases of legal kidnapping, since this process involves convincing the legislators to do their job and put new laws on the books protecting parents. Many lawmakers have forgotten that their main job is to serve the people and carry out the will of the people. The government works for its citizens, so if enough citizens demand change, then the government must listen. When citizens exercise their rights, they can spur lawmakers to action and remind them of the rights guaranteed by the Constitution.

One big problem standing in the way of rooting out the corruption in CPS is that the corruption has extended to the courts. Many judges are under the thumb of the government, as are attorneys, all of which work together to take kids away from their parents. It is often impossible to have your complaints with the system heard, because too often judges will simply throw the case out, or agree with CPS without ever truly listening to your side. If this corruption is to end, it's clear that the courts aren't the way to do it. The people need to bypass the courts and go right to the laws of the land so their cases aren't being blocked, and one of the best ways to accomplish this is through affidavits.

The Role of Judges and Attorneys

In an ideal world, every parent whose children are taken away by CPS would have the right to a fair trial. This is guaranteed in the U.S. Constitution's Bill of Rights. Despite this, many parents find that when they go to court to argue their case for custody of their kids, the trial is less than fair. They may face opposition from the attorney on the side of the state, their own attorney, and even the judge presiding over the case. This is unfortunate, but also unsurprising when you consider who stands to benefit from kids getting taken away from parents. If judges and attorneys are also getting kickbacks from the government for taking kids, they are more likely to side with CPS, and less likely to listen to parents' stories of how their rights were violated.

To eliminate the flaws in the system, it's necessary to address not just the laws governing the actions of CPS, but also those governing the attorneys and judges in charge of these cases. It's no secret that many parent and family advocacy groups have butted heads with judges in the past over these exact issues. For example, in 2018 the group Parents Against CPS Corruption (PACC) demanded the removal of three judges from the Contra Costa Superior Court. PACC alleged that the judges were "routinely violating" the civil and constitutional rights of litigants" as they "ignored evidence and apparently made pre-determined rulings based on relationships between them and certain local lawyers" (Tully & Weiss, n.d., para. 2). In particular, the three judges were accused of placing kids with unfit foster families that put children in greater danger, ignoring the Welfare and Institutions Code in favor of separating families, and referring parents to lawyers who would not only purposefully lose their cases, but who would also drive the families to the brink of bankruptcy with exorbitant fees. The very next year, another judge not involved in the initial allegations but who presided over the same court was removed from the bench for acts of both willful and prejudicial misconduct. These cases make up just a fraction of the judicial corruption that parents face when they are trying to keep their families together, but they are a symptom of a nation-wide problem that puts judges on the side of CPS.

Teaching the Law Through Affidavits

As a result of these corrupt judges and others like them, parents have lost faith in the ability of the courts to reunite them with their kids. If the judges are working in favor of CPS, it wouldn't be much of a stretch to suggest these same judges would throw out any allegations of CPS misconduct that violate parents' and kids' rights, nor would they seriously consider challenges to laws like Title 42. Instead, the push for change must come from the people. Through writing affidavits and putting testimony of corruption on the record, more people learn about the problem, and more people demand change from their local and federal governments.

You may not believe you have a lot of political power as an average citizen, but in truth, you have more than you know. Many people refer to the United States' system of government as a democracy, but this isn't completely accurate. In a democracy, people have a say, but only in how they elect representatives who then go on to make the laws themselves. But when you look at the founding of the country, you see that everyday people were the ones to make the laws and lay the groundwork for the nations' future. The common man has always had control over the laws of the country. The founding fathers were farmers and regular citizens before they took a leading role in shaping the U.S., and even then, many of the most notable early lawmakers were almost entirely self-taught. Therefore, it is more accurate to call America a common law republic. This means everything that goes on within the country is governed by its laws and founding documents, like the federal Constitution, Bill of Rights, and state Constitutions. At the end of the day, the people make the laws, not the judges or other elected officials. There is a reason why the preamble begins with the phrase "We the people," and it is because the average citizens have always had the highest authority in the land. If the people want to change these laws and get rid of ones that violate the Constitution, like Title 42, they only need to exercise their authority as granted to them by the Constitution itself.

It's easy to see the power people wield when they work together, whether they are fighting against CPS or other forms of government corruption. You only need to look as far as the most recent election, when groups of citizens across the country declared their right to conduct an audit of the electoral votes to ensure only legal votes were being counted. This was a movement led by the people, and thanks to affidavits, many states have engaged in electoral audits in an effort to uncover the truth of the 2020 election. What some don't know is that the election audit process started in Maricopa, Arizona, as a direct result of David and Josh working with the people to send out affidavits.

The Maricopa Audit

In the wake of the 2020 election, many voters, typically those who were registered as Republicans, shared stories of unusual occurrences at the polling booths. Some reported seeing bags and boxes filled with ballots entering and leaving the polling stations at unusual times. Others claimed that they tried to vote normally, filling out their ballots with a pen, but they were only given magic markers, which would have bled through and voided the ballots. The majority of these situations happened on the day of the election, when most Republicans went to the polls, as opposed to Democratic votes which largely arrived through early voting and mail-in ballots. If these stories were true, their implications were clear: there were people at the polling stations trying to suppress Republican voting, all in an effort to steal the election.

The more frequent these claims became, the more public outcry grew. People wanted to know if the election results were genuine, or if there was a greater scheme going on to remove President Trump from office at any cost, even if it meant undermining the will of the American people. With so many stories, it was natural that people had their doubts about how any election could be considered fair when one side was being targeted, harassed, and prevented from voting. Luckily, as more and more people started to doubt the election results and voice their concerns, David and Josh knew the results could be double-checked through the use of an audit.

Gathering Testimony

When election fraud occurs, it is difficult if not impossible for outsiders to the system to prove it. After all, the people don't have access to the ballots, and election fraud can be effectively unable to be detected when you're not in the room counting the votes. Luckily, in order to question the results of an election and request an audit, you don't have to have evidence of fraud. You only need to prove that maladministration of ballots has occurred.

Maladministration refers to any actions taken by a government or government official that are corrupt, or that cause injustice. When people went to the polls and were forced to use markers that bled through the thin ballot sheets, this was maladministration. When voters were unable to submit their legal votes for any reason, and when illegally cast votes that should have been thrown out were counted, these were acts of maladministration as well. As the Arizona Constitution states, "All elections shall be free and equal, and no power, civil or military, shall at any time interfere to prevent the free exercise of the right of suffrage" (Arizona Const. art. II, pt. 21). When maladministration occurs, the election is by definition no longer free and equal, and the results can be called into question through an audit and investigation.

Thousands of people in Arizona claimed to have witnessed acts of maladministration when they attempted to vote, which indicates that there is a high likelihood that fraud could have occurred, and the election could have been stolen. David and Josh set up a booth in Maricopa and invited people to come share what they experienced at the polls, good and bad. They asked people to sign affidavits affirming their testimony to help get the word out about what was happening, just like they used affidavits against CPS. As word spread, the demand for a full audit to be conducted grew, and the people asserted their right to have the ballots recounted to ensure a fair election. Audit requests do not have to be approved by the courts, nor do they require proof of fraud. The affidavits simply helped inform Arizona residents and people across the country about what was going on, including lawmakers who could assist in the auditing efforts.

As always, the push must come from the people, not the courts. Many courts were rejecting claims of potential voter fraud without even holding proper trials, silencing the public. But in truth, the court's support wasn't necessary. The state Senate can launch an investigation into an election that must be free from executive and judicial interference if they feel compelled to do so, and the thousands of affidavits pouring in were especially compelling. It wasn't long before Arizona's electoral audit began, helmed by the private firm Cyber Ninjas to ensure the government could not interfere.

What would come to be known as the Maricopa County presidential ballot audit was a never-before-seen occurrence.

For the first time in history, the people banded together to push for an electoral audit that could potentially have the power to overturn election results. Arizona had become ground zero for the movement to reinstate President Trump, and it wasn't long before other states took notice.

Spread Through the Country

The audit in Maricopa was far from the only one to occur in the wake of the 2020 election results. People suspected fraud all around the country, which led to more and more demands for audits. Many states used the affidavit method popularized by David and Josh. Every day, new audits seemed to be popping up in various states including Pennsylvania, Wisconsin, Michigan, Texas, and more. The message was clear: the people wanted to know the truth, and they were willing to exercise their rights to learn it. They were inspired by the work David and Josh were doing in Maricopa, and they took action in their own states.

Over time, even some government officials were brought on as allies to the cause. As a candidate for election to the House of Representatives himself, Josh had the opportunity to speak directly with many other political candidates and determine which ones were sympathetic to the cause. These included Army Colonel Phil Waldron, a cybersecurity expert who helped bring the issue to the notice of the Arizona State legislature. Josh also worked to convince doubters of the truth of election fraud claims. Notably, he arranged a meeting with Board of Supervisors member Steve Chucri, and after extensive discussions he convinced Chucri to vote in favor of the audit. While Chucri was the only member of the Board of Supervisors to do so, this was still a significant step forward, as it proved just how serious the movement was getting for legislators to take notice and change their opinions to work toward the common good. Josh's outreach efforts also included a meeting with President Trump's attorney Rudy Giuliani, all of which helped to legitimize the claims of election fraud in the American peoples' eyes.

The affidavit movement even made it all the way to Hawaii, through the work of Pastor Junior Tupai. Tupai delivered a stirring presentation in October of 2021 about how affidavits can be used to give the people more control over their government, showcasing how they allow average citizens to instruct their elected officials to work for them, not the other way around. During his speech, Tupai thanked David and Josh for all the hard work they were doing getting the word out and fighting back against fraud in Maricopa, using their work as inspiration for his own efforts to introduce people to the affidavit and audit movement in Hawaii.

Everywhere, across the nation, the people were the ones demanding change. The people demanded more from their representatives, and they demanded that those in positions of power take action and lend their support to the movement. The Maricopa audit made it clear to many that it isn't necessary to involve the courts to approve a request for an audit. Instead, the people were granted power by the law to question the validity of the election results, and American citizens learned that they could fight against corruption using the Constitution as their guide.

Grand Juries

Another ally to the cause was Kandiss Taylor, a candidate running for governor of Georgia who was referred to Josh through Lin Wood, a lawyer who fought against illegal ballot certification after the election. Wood had caught wind of the push for affidavits and audits in Arizona, and he believed Taylor could assist in sparking the same audits in Georgia. After learning about what Josh and David were doing to give the people their power back, Taylor quickly joined the cause herself as a vocal supporter. She collected thousands of affidavits in Georgia, which drew a significant amount of attention from government officials. It wasn't long before Georgia officials were showing up at the Maricopa audit, looking to learn more about the process and hear David and Josh out. Soon after, a big push for an audit was launched in

Georgia as well, and Taylor worked toward bringing the case to the attention of the grand jury.

Grand juries are populated by average, everyday citizens rather than potentially corrupt judges. The people get the power to listen to all of the evidence and arguments, and use this information to form their own opinions to determine the outcome of a case. This eliminates the possibility of judges and attorneys working to protect themselves, each other, and their government allies. In many cases, district attorneys act as 'bouncers' meant to keep the common peoples' complaints out of the courts. These complaints rarely make it to the courtroom, and when they do, the verdict is often up to the judge, who may already have a verdict in mind before anyone has had a chance to say a single word.

Grand juries, on the other hand, give everyone a fair chance to be listened to and have their evidence and testimony weighed against the opposing side. Government officials who would otherwise be protected can be held accountable for their actions, which have been described in affidavits. These affidavits prove that corrupt officials acted illegally, were informed what they were doing was wrong, and still failed to change their ways. They serve as more than enough proof for most juries, which is why the courts are so afraid of giving people access to grand jury trials. As a result, it may come as no surprise that American citizens have routinely faced obstacles when trying to bring claims of election maladministration and other cases in front of grand juries.

Some have tried to argue that these cases are too serious to have their verdicts decided by regular people. This logic doesn't hold up when you consider that murder cases, which can often carry lifetime sentences, are decided upon by a grand jury. If we can trust the people to make potentially life-altering decisions during murder trials, why can't we trust them to judge matters like election fraud and misconduct by government officials? The truth is that by restricting the use of grand juries, this is just one more way by which the government attempts to restrict the power of the people, and it cannot be allowed to continue.

The Purpose of Audits

There is a mistaken belief from critics of the electoral audits that if the vote count remains the same, then the audit will have failed. However, this just isn't true. Firstly, all audits provide valuable information about an election, whether they confirm or oppose the initial results. Performing an audit is a win-win situation. Either no fraud is found, which ensures that U.S. elections are functioning as intended, or evidence of fraud is uncovered through the recount, which could change the election results while also drawing attention to the flaws in the current system so they can be corrected. Ideally, if the audits show evidence of fraud and prove that in a fair election President Trump would have won, then there is Constitutional basis for Trump to resume his presidency. Even if there isn't enough evidence to prove fraud, everyone who has involved themselves in the auditing process by writing affidavits or even just watching coverage of the situation has learned something new about their rights.

Additionally, these audits aren't just about flipping the electoral verdict of certain states. They are also about making the maladministration at the polling booths known to as many people as possible. Everyone who agrees to sign an affidavit can make their voice heard, and together, they can expose avenues for fraud that interfere with the counting of legal votes. No matter what the results of election audits are, there is a net gain for the American people, as they provide the public with information they might have otherwise never heard. The people recognize that they have the power and the right to correct problems with the way their government is run, wherever these problems may occur. They now know that the process for voting can change, and that they can have a hand in demanding these changes to ensure the security of all elections. They also know which government officials were willing to listen and investigate claims of voter fraud, and which ones were willing to suppress these claims for the sake of remaining in a position of power. This empowers people to take action and fight for change, whether this means pressuring their local lawmakers to address corruption or fighting for their rights as citizens in the face of overbearing masking, vaccination, and quarantine mandates popularized during the COVID-19 pandemic.

Chapter 6

Defending Against Other Forms of Government Overreach

"Intoxicated with unbroken success, we have become too self-sufficient to feel the necessity of redeeming and preserving grace, too proud to pray to the God that made us."

Abraham Lincoln

The corruption of CPS is a serious issue, but it's just one symptom of the problems that currently plague our government. When the government works against the people rather than for them, you get policies that don't respect the rights of citizens. One such policy that's been a popular topic of conversation lately are the federal and local government mandates related to the virus COVID-19. While these mandates claim to be in our best interest, they carry serious consequences that prevent people from being able to provide for their families and make important decisions about their own health.

Masking, vaccination, and quarantine mandates all infringe upon the rights of the people and take away our freedoms. The steps you take to protect your health should be your personal choice, but the government has stepped in and decided what to do for you, interfering with your right to choose. When you catch a cold, you have the right to decide if you want to go to your doctor and take prescription medicine, pick up something over-the-counter, use natural remedies, or just wait for your body to fight it off naturally. No one comes into your home and demands you wear a mask, but thanks to COVID-19 mandates, this is exactly the type of challenge people face when they want to make their own decisions about how they treat and prevent illness. Similar issues arise with mandated vaccines, especially since the vaccines used to prevent the spread of COVID-19 are so new, and many families believe they aren't safe. Without submitting to getting a vaccine, you may be unable to work, which means you can't put food on the table. These mandates restrict where you can go and what you can do if you disagree with the way the government wants you to handle your own health, effectively denying you many of your Constitutionally-guaranteed freedoms.

Many COVID-19 mandates end up harming children, just like corruption in CPS. Young kids are expected to wear masks in schools and in public places, as well as for long flights on airplanes. These mandates are in place regardless of what you as a parent think is best for your child, even though you have the right to ask for second opinions and refuse medical procedures and treatments you think would be harmful. In most school districts, kids are also expected to be vaccinated to attend school and do extracurricular activities like sports and clubs. However, the districts and local governments writing these laws may know very little, if anything at all, about how safe COVID-19 vaccines are for children, especially their long-term effects. In both cases, the health and safety of children is deemed less important than following a mandate which benefits the government and has the potential to harm your family, as do the problems with CPS.

One of the most significant issues with COVID-19 mandates interfering with the rights of the people is when quarantine and shutdown mandates force businesses to close. For many who run these businesses, they are their livelihood, and they can't afford to pay their bills without them. Even a closure of a few months could spell disaster for the majority of small-business owners. As a result of government bullying, if these businesses are forced to abide by shutdown mandates, they may end up being unable to keep the business open. This in turn leads to small-business owners struggling to keep up with rent and mortgage payments, ending up deeper and deeper in debt as shutdown continues and they have no recourse by which to reopen their business.

However, while a shutdown mandate can seem like the end of the world, there are ways to fight back against it, just like you can fight back against masking and vaccination mandates. While thousands of businesses have been shuttered as a result of shutdowns, some business owners have managed to reopen even during shutdown to continue providing their vital services to customers and bringing in money for their families. Such was the case for Josh, who learned how to fight back and keep his gym open in the face of serious opposition from the state government.

The Story of Josh's Gym

In March of 2020, fears of the COVID-19 virus led many governments across the country to completely shut down their states. This meant restaurants were relegated to only being able to serve take-out, severely cutting into their profits; devout church-goers were unable to attend weekly services; and thousands of businesses were deemed non-essential and required to close completely. Like many other states, Arizona also implemented these guidelines, which meant that Josh was expected to close the gym he owned and ran, MetroFlex. Of course, it wasn't so easy for Josh to just close up shop. After all, his income was tied to his gym, and on top of that, many of his customers relied on the gym to keep themselves healthy and in shape. If he allowed his gym to close, he would have jeopardized not only his family's well-being, but also the well-being of many members of the community.

Despite this, government pressure to close continued to mount. Josh kept his MetroFlex open for two weeks after the shutdown mandate took effect. During this time, he faced increasing opposition from officials as well as legal threats. He knew these attempts to force his business to close were unconstitutional, and that they interfered with his rights as a business owner and as a private citizen. However, what he didn't know was how to fight back against them and avoid the mandates. Due to all the pressure from government officials, MetroFlex closed its doors, but they wouldn't stay that way for long. It was only about a week and a half before the gym was welcoming new and old customers alike once again.

Josh found the solution to his problem when he spoke to David about the effects the shutdown mandates were having on his business. He knew he couldn't stay closed for long, so together, Josh and David designed a plan that would help the gym reopen without violating any laws, so the government would not be able to force Josh to shut down again. This was accomplished through the use of private membership associations (PMAs), which afford businesses additional rights, even in the face of unconstitutional mandates. By using PMAs to their advantage, Josh and David were able to turn the tables and declare their rights. In fact, not only were they able to help their own business, but they were also able to provide guidance and assistance to other gyms in the area that were struggling to stay open during shutdown orders. Altogether, over a hundred businesses were saved through this powerful strategy.

If you're a business owner or if you know someone who is, you're already aware of just how devastating the COVID-19 mandates are to many businesses that are not deemed essential. Fighting these mandates is just like fighting corruption in CPS. It's a community-led movement that anyone can be a part of, regardless of how much experience they have in political and legal matters. Declaring your rights as a business owner, or helping others in your community do the same, starts with learning about PMAs and the benefits they provide.

Private Membership Associations

When most people start a business as an individual or with a partner, they are advised to mark their business as a

Limited Liability Company (LLC). An LLC is a type of business structure that helps to protect your money. As the name implies, an LLC limits your liability if your business gets into hot water. For example, if you owe a significant amount of money and you have to declare bankruptcy, the business is treated as a separate financial entity from yourself. You don't have to delve into your own pockets to pay off your business' expenses, and creditors cannot garnish your wages from a different job to pay for debts owed by the business. Because it offers business owners so many protections, an LLC is one of the most common types of companies for small business owners. However, in some cases, there are other types of business categorizations that offer better protections. During COVID-19 shutdowns, PMAs rose to prominence as struggling business owners fought to reopen their stores, and they have helped over 110 small businesses across the country regain their footing during a period of serious economic uncertainty.

To understand exactly what PMA is and how it may be able to help you, start by looking at the name. 'Private' means that PMA businesses are not considered public buildings like many other storefronts. They typically have a dedicated group of clientele that frequent the store, and there may be an application process for people who want to become customers. This is where the 'membership' aspect comes into play. Clients of these businesses are considered members, and the members are allowed to spend their time on private property with rules determined by the business owner. This is key, as it is what prevents PMA businesses from having to follow many COVID-19 mandates. While the government can regulate what people do in public spaces, like criminalizing the simple act of not wearing a mask, they cannot do the same for what you do in your home, nor does their reach extend to any private property. By operating your business as a PMA, you designate your property as private, so you get to make the rules and invite your members in when you please.

Finally, PMAs involve an aspect of 'association' that provides them with distinct legal rights when compared to a standard company. In particular, associations are granted freedoms under the first amendment under the right to assemble. Therefore, associations are not subject to laws that would restrict their ability to meet in violation of their constitutional rights. What this means for you, as a business owner or someone who wants to support small businesses, is that even COVID-19 shutdown mandates cannot prevent people from meeting in your association.

There is another important aspect of PMAs to keep in mind, and this is that they are closely tied to health stores, gyms, natural food stores, and other businesses related to achieving and maintaining good physical and mental fitness. In other words, a PMA can be seen as a method by which people are "collectively asserting and standing upon their rights to determine what devices, products, procedures, or services will be used by them to maintain the health of their own body, mind or spirit" (Private Membership Associations Common-Law Trusts, n.d., para. 11). As mentioned previously, you get to determine what treatment methods and procedures you and your family get, and the government should not be able to restrict your access to them. Therefore, if a family decides they want to go to the gym to maintain their health, even during COVID-19 shutdowns, through the power of the PMA, they can. PMAs have allowed countless businesses to reopen in spite of government ordinances, and they have been truly indispensable tools for the small business owners like Josh who have been able to make use of them.

Who Can Declare Their Business a PMA

The PMA categorization is incredibly useful, but it's important to remember that it's only applicable to certain kinds of businesses. This is because the point of PMAs is to empower people to make their own choices about their health and well-being. Therefore, businesses that choose to label themselves as PMAs generally must have something to do with the health and fitness sector. Of course, this covers many different kinds of businesses, including those that you may not initially suspect would fall under the categorization.

Most types of healthcare providers can qualify for PMA status, as they provide medical services. This includes independent doctors and nurses, midwives, doulas, chiropractors, mental health professionals, and dentists. It can also include massage therapists and those who invent or sell methods for reducing pain, swelling, inflammation, and illness in their patients. Those who own gyms and other workout facilities can establish their business as a PMA, as can owners of health food stores. Even churches and other religious groups can be protected under PMA categorization, as they support the health of the mind and soul. So while PMAs are primarily focused on protecting those in the healthcare sector, they can be applicable to many different types of businesses that need protection, so long as these businesses are considered private memberships.

Private Versus Public Businesses

PMAs allow business owners to recategorize their businesses under the label of private entities, which afford them greater protections. They are not subject to following the same rules that public business owners must abide by, so most PMAs will be able to reopen during COVID-19 shutdowns without issue. But what exactly does it mean to be considered private, and how does it differ from more public-facing businesses?

Private associations involve members coming together to accomplish a common goal. This goal can be improving their health, sharing a sense of community, worshipping, and gathering. Private associations typically have members who routinely meet at the association, and they may have membership dues similar to gym membership or health club fees, though this is not mandatory. These associations are considered private to protect political groups, advocates, and others meeting together to help inspire change, so long as the meetings are held on privately owned property, where the government does not have the same jurisdiction it has for public entities.

In many states throughout the country, private associations are afforded far greater protections than LLCs, corporations, and other types of public businesses. For example, protections for associations are baked right into Arizona's Executive Orders for COVID-19 guidelines. Simply look at the Arizona legislature, specifically the Arizona Revised Statutes (A.R.S.) under section 26-317. It first states, "Any person who violates any provision of this chapter or who knowingly fails or refuses to obey any lawful order or regulation issued as provided in this chapter," meaning anyone found to be in knowing violation of shutdown guidelines, "shall be guilty of a class 1 misdemeanor" (A.R.S., § 26–317). This is what typically provides the state with power to send police in to forcibly shut down your business if you refuse to comply with Governor Doug Ducey's mandates, and it means you can be heavily fined and risk losing your business. However, the same law also states, "This provision does not apply to the refusal of any private organization or member thereof to participate in a local emergency or state of emergency" (A.R.S., § 26–317). Private organizations and associations can continue to meet, as the law threatening their businesses does not apply to them. Because you are categorized as a private organization, you cannot be controlled in the same way as public businesses.

Despite what critics may believe, this isn't just a flimsy excuse for people to ignore government regulations. Instead, it is part of a long history of people using associations to defend their rights and freedoms, and it has clear ties to various cases fought in state Supreme Courts. In particular, PMAs have long been a tool used by civil rights organizations to guarantee their right to assembly. In 1958, the state of Alabama attempted to prevent members of the NAACP from meeting and conducting their business within the state. However, this was a clear violation of the first amendment's guarantee of the right to assemble. Alabama state courts attempted to issue a restraining order and a subpoena for membership lists, but the NAACP took their case to the supreme court, arguing that their rights had been violated. In particular, they alleged that Alabama had violated the rights guaranteed by the fourteenth amendment, which states that no state shall "deprive any person of life, liberty, or property, without due process of law" (U.S. Const. amend. XIV, § 2).

The court found that "immunity from state scrutiny of petitioner's membership lists is here so related to the right of petitioner's members to pursue their lawful private interests privately and to associate freely with others in doing so," and that the "freedom to associate with organizations dedicated to the 'advancement of beliefs and ideas' is an inseparable part of the Due Process Clause of the Fourteenth Amendment" (Oyez, n.d., para. 3). In other words, the ruling ensured that the government could not interfere with the NAACP's right to organize by demanding a list of its members to intimidate, harass, or otherwise discourage them from continuing to meet.

This is a landmark case for anyone who supports the right to assemble, especially for businesses that are considered private associations. People have a right to carry out their lawful private interests on their own property without interference from the government. Your business is protected in the same way. Since you are categorizing your business as a PMA, it is a private organization, and thus you and your customers have the right to continue to meet. Should anyone question you, remind them that you have the law on your side, and hold firm to your beliefs. Once you reopen as a PMA, the government should not be able to force you to shut down again, as these rights are protected by both supreme court case precedent and the Constitution itself.

Constitutional Protection

If you are a small business owner struggling to maintain your livelihood, remember that the law is on your side. While new mandates and emergency guidelines may be in direct opposition to your goals, the laws of the land are not, and you can use them to your advantage. Start by returning to your state's constitution and checking out what it has to say about the rights of private citizens using their own property to assemble. The Arizona State Constitution has specific guarantees that protect citizens from unwarranted government interference. Article 2, Section 8 of the Arizona Constitution is titled the "Right to Privacy," and it states that "No person shall be disturbed in his private affairs, or his home invaded, without authority of law" (Arizona Const. art. II, pt. 8). If you are not conducting illegal business in your store, gym, or company, the government does not have the authority to invade it or tell you to shut down operations. After all, you are not committing any wrongdoing just by operating, since this is protected for PMAs. The only case in which the government can interfere is if you are presenting a clear and present danger to the members of your PMA through purposefully life-threatening actions, which should not apply so long as you are operating legally. Therefore, there is no need for the government to send anyone to disturb you, or to harass you or your clientele for remaining open.

Many people don't know about the protections the law affords them, which is what makes these laws so powerful. Once you know about them and you use them to defend yourself against those who would see your business closed for good, you can stand up for yourself and for others in your community. Many small business owners had police officers showing up at their doors, trying to serve them warrants or fines because they remained open during the shutdown. These owners felt threatened and bullied into complying, even though they didn't have to. Since you have the law on your side, you know that the government cannot interfere with your PMA in this way, and you can remain open. Once Josh declared his rights and fought to keep his gym open, he no longer has to deal with pressure, harassment, and legal threats. In fact, the only cops who showed up were ones who wanted to sign up for a gym membership.

How to Make Your Business a PMA

At this point, you know all the benefits that being a PMA provides for your business and your income, which in turn supports your family. However, you may not know exactly how to turn your business into a PMA so you can reopen.

Luckily, you just have to follow a few simple and easy steps and you'll be on your way to reopening in no time. These steps include making sure you meet the qualifications, notifying the government of the change in status of your business, and declaring your rights through an affidavit.

If you want to fast-track your business into a PMA so you can reopen as quickly as possible, it's a good idea to enlist help from experts who have been through the process before. David offers services that assist struggling small business owners with completing and submitting the relevant paperwork, as well as creating and sending in affidavits to protect businesses from being forcibly closed. Whether you want to navigate your way through the process alone or you prefer to take advantage of these services, it's still important to understand the basic steps. This will prevent you from being taken advantage of by bad attorneys who only want to extend their billable hours as long as possible. Some will promise to help you reclassify your business, only to end up dragging the matter out into extensive courtroom battles. You want to follow the most direct path so you don't end up overpaying for these services, which means sticking to the most effective method: qualify, notify, and declare.

Qualify

First and foremost, before you can pursue turning your business into a PMA, you must meet the qualifications. While many businesses can fit under the umbrella of either health care facilities or private associations working together to accomplish a goal, some may have to take a more unique approach to reopening if the business cannot be easily tied into one of the protected types of practices. Don't let this deter you though. If you're unsure if your business would qualify, seek out the assistance of an expert like David, who will review your case and determine if a PMA is right for you. If not, there may be another path for you to take to ensure reopening is still a possibility, and a well-versed expert will be able to guide you through an alternate approach.

Notify

Once you have decided to turn your business into a PMA, you must complete the necessary paperwork to do so. You will need to fill out the association articles and documents needed to recategorize your business. These forms notify the government that your association is no longer subject to their guidelines, so you should have no further legal issues once all of the paperwork is sorted. The protocol for this change and the exact forms needed differ depending on the state where you live. You can acquire these forms from online PMA advocacy groups, or work with the assistance of someone experienced in establishing PMAs to help guide you through filling them out and filing them with the appropriate offices in your state.

Declare

After submitting the paperwork, all that's left is for you to stick to your guns and defend yourself from continued government attempts at interference. The most effective way to accomplish this is through affidavits. As previously covered in Chapter 4, an affidavit is a document that can be used as your sworn testimony, just like when you are under oath in a courtroom. It is an official legal statement declaring that everything you say is, to the best of your knowledge, completely factual. Affidavits allow you to declare your rights and protect your freedoms if you face future opposition from the government, making them invaluable tools. Experienced PMA experts like David can assist you with writing and sending affidavits to ensure no one tries to shut your business down again. These are services that few if any attorneys would provide, given that you might have to send out affidavits year-round to prevent the government from continuing to attack your business, which is why so many business owners

JOSH BARNETT & DAVID JOSE

trust David and Josh to help them get their businesses back up and running.

Once you have completed the PMA process, you are ready to reopen your business as a private entity. Within your building, you are free to gather and set the rules as you see fit. Of course, these rules only extend to the borders of your property. For other overreaching COVID-19 regulations that can harm individuals and families, like vaccination and mask mandates, you will need to take a different approach to keep yourself and your family safe.

Handling Mask Mandates

Mask mandates are another method through which the government has used COVID-19 as an excuse to push their own agenda. Wearing a mask and getting vaccinated are personal decisions that everyone should be able to make for themselves, like getting a flu shot each year or deciding whether or not to wear a scarf when it's cold. The government can't force you to make these kinds of healthcare decisions, yet with masking and vaccination mandates, this is exactly what they are trying to achieve.

As a citizen, you have the right to decide how you protect yourself. This right is guaranteed under the Constitution, and state and federal mandates that go against this are unconstitutional. Of course, it is not so easy to fight this kind of regulation as an individual on such a grand scale. Until the mask mandates are lifted, most businesses will attempt to comply with them whether the owners agree or not out of fear of being shut down. You can choose to avoid businesses that enforce a masking or vaccination policy, but it is not always so easy. This is especially true in the case of kids being forced to wear masks in schools, where they cannot simply stay home without putting their education at risk. As a result, masking in schools has become a very divisive issue, with thousands of concerned parents taking to town hall meetings and forums to fight for their kids' rights to keep the government out of their personal healthcare decisions.

Masking In Schools

Many schools across the country have instituted mask mandates for their students. Kids are expected to wear a mask the whole time they are in school. At best, these masks are distracting and uncomfortable for many students. They should be focusing on learning, but instead they have one more thing to worry about, which could be distracting them from their education. At worst, many believe that masks can harm the wearers' health, and that students should not be subjected to these mandates out of concern for their well-being. Wherever you happen to fall on this issue, the law is clear: taking healthcare decisions out of the hands of the parent and putting them in the hands of the state is unconstitutional.

Just like in cases of medical kidnapping, school mask mandates violate your right to make decisions about your child's health and wellness. The state should not be making these choices, nor should the federal government. Parents, who know what is best for their children, should not have their rights infringed upon by governments looking to mask kids for entire school days, and protesting these decisions should not be a reason for the government to act against your wishes as a parent or, worse, to threaten to take your kids away. Remember that the law is on your side. The Arizona State Constitution supports parents' rights to make healthcare decisions for their kids, as do many other State Constitutions across the nation.

Even though most schools believe they have to comply with federal regulations, this just isn't true. In fact, according to the Constitution, these laws are actually unenforceable. When reviewing mask mandates, the Congressional Research Center found that "the Supreme Court has interpreted the Tenth Amendment to prevent the federal government from commandeering or requiring state officers to carry out federal directives. This principle thus prevents Congress from requiring states or localities to mandate masks" (Congressional Research Center, 2020, p. 3). While the government can incentivize its citizens to make certain choices in the service of public health, regulations passed at a federal level do not have to be enforced by the state, and they certainly don't have to be enforced by school administrators. This means that to fight back against school mask mandates, you don't have to take on the federal government; you just have to speak to your school board. COVID-19 mandates are still being hotly contested across the country, with some states upholding and attempting to enforce the mandates while others explicitly outlaw them. One thing is for certain: these mandates are not set in stone. You can fight for your right to determine your child's medical treatments, including masking and vaccinations, and in many cases, parents have succeeded in doing so.

All the same, many school boards are the ones providing the greatest resistance to parents who want to protect their children, even when the state may not mandate masks or vaccinations in schools. Again, it's important to look at where the money is going. Financial incentives for vaccinations have led many schools to push for them, uncaring of how many parents decide to pull their children. After all, they may be making more money off mandating vaccinations and getting Title 42 payouts for medical kidnapping cases than they get from enrollment. Finances and greed are being put above child welfare, and it cannot be allowed to continue.

If you find yourself at odds with your child's school administrators, make your voice as a parent heard. Alone, you may not be able to convince your school to drop their mask mandates, since they are facing a lot of pressure from the government to keep these mandates in place. When you work together with other parents, however, you can fight for real change within the schools, protecting your kids and ensuring they can focus on their education without potentially risking their health to conform to mask and vaccination mandates.

Affidavit Mommas

In the wake of COVID-19 masking and vaccination mandates, parents have to rely on each other for support and advocacy now more than ever. Many parents across the country have banded together to fight back against their district school boards, primarily through using affidavits. As always, affidavits remain very useful tools, especially when large groups of people band together and make their voices heard. These parents have become known as affidavit mommas, and the pressure they've put on school boards has gone a long way toward halting and reversing the adoption of mask mandates in schools.

While the fight still continues, the affidavit mommas are proof that affidavits really do work, and that they can empower you and your fellow parents to stand up for what is right. Just like business owners who cannot afford to shut down, parents can make use of affidavits to tell the people in charge that they know the law, and they will not back down until their rights are respected. When everyone is working together, the people have the power, and they are better equipped to keep their families safe.

Chapter 7

Returning the Power to the People

"The Bible is the rock on which our Republic rests."

Andrew Jackson

The affidavit movement and the fight against CPS corruption is, at its core, a grassroots movement. It has always been led by the people and for the people. Its leaders are not career politicians or famous attorneys, but instead regular guys who have taken the initiative to learn the law and utilize it for positive change. Because the movement is led by the people, this has led many opportunists to set their sights on it and try to rise to the top. However, this sets a dangerous precedent. Many of the people attempting to infiltrate the movement only took interest in it when it grew in popularity, which indicates they might be more motivated by a desire for improving their public opinion than a wish to help people. Others pretend to support the movement, but they may really be trying to take it down from the inside. In either case, power is being wrested away from the people, which goes against the core of the movement.

It's important to be wary of big-name figures who swoop in and try to make the movement all about themselves. They may seem harmless, but many of these infiltrators have ulterior motives that only ever stand in the way of people who are serious about accomplishing their goals, whether these goals are helping to return kids taken by CPS or pushing back against unconstitutional COVID-19 mandates. It's important to keep the movement on track, and that means not allowing yourself to be swayed by people who would serve their own interests rather than serving the interests of the people.

Remember that at its core, the affidavit movement is about empowering everyday citizens to do the right thing. Anyone who wants to use the movement for their own gain doesn't care about the people, and they certainly don't care about saving the state of the nation. Doing the right thing requires teamwork, transparency, and honesty, so always be wary of those looking to make the movement about themselves rather than giving back to the communities that gave them their power and influence in the first place.

The Danger of Infiltrators

In a movement led by the people, it is critical that every member is devoted to the cause and working with the same set of information. One of the most significant dangers that can occur when infiltrators find their way into the group is that a previously unified front of parents, business owners, and concerned citizens suddenly starts to fracture into different camps, all fighting for different things. Maybe one group wants to handle CPS corruption through affidavits, while another is convinced that change has to come from working through the courts. Trying to pursue both methods for change at the same time only wastes resources, pulling them away from the solutions that actually work like affidavits and diverting them toward wastes of time. This can lead to fights within the group, which only stalls the movement and ensures no one can make any progress, allowing the corruption to continue.

Some infiltrators can also make the movement as a whole look bad. They might express fringe views that few people in the group really believe, all while claiming to speak for the entire group. If just one person believes in a provably false narrative and spreads lies, it realistically shouldn't taint the group as a whole. However, when that one person is very vocal about their beliefs and they claim to be a leader within the movement, even when they don't have the support of the majority of the people, they can get the whole group labeled as conspiracy theorists. People who have never heard of the corruption in CPS before might decide it's all untrue just because they don't believe what one or two people are saying. This is why it's important to carefully consider who you listen to, as not everyone has your best interests at heart.

They might even be purposefully trying to make the movement look bad, which makes it harder for everyone else to be taken seriously when they fight for change.

Finally, infiltrators can often overshadow the people actually trying to supply the group with real, valuable information. Many would-be infiltrators are just in it for the money, and they don't really care about the success of the movement. They aren't really interested in helping distraught parents piece their families back together, nor do they really care about small business owners who are worried about how they will feed their families if they can't reopen their businesses. They promise that they have all the answers, but they aren't interested in educating people about how to write audits or take action within their communities. They don't offer any real solutions, and it's the people who suffer and lose hope as a result.

Identifying Infiltrators

At this point, it should be clear that infiltrators can pose a huge threat to the ability of the movement to get things done. But how can you tell the difference between someone who really cares about the movement and someone who is just here to serve their own self interests? First, it's important to always keep an eye out and consider information critically. If someone promises things that are too good to be true, it's good practice to doubt these claims until you see for yourself that they really work. Other tip-offs that indicate someone might not be on the up-and-up include having a poor or spotty track record, failing to provide actual guidance, and taking control away from the people.

Not everyone who ends up being an infiltrator will have a public track record of where they stand on issues like mask mandates and CPS corruption, but for those who do, it's important to consider their previous stances before you decide to listen to what they have to say. If someone was very vocally protesting the idea that affidavits work only a few months ago, and then all of the sudden changed their tune when they started trying to infiltrate the movement, this is a good sign that they might not be as genuine as they seem. This isn't to say that no one can ever change their mind. There are many people who started out as doubters but who have become genuine allies of the movement over time. This is perfectly fine; it doesn't always matter what someone did in the past as long as they are willing to take steps to fix it today. However, there's a big difference between someone who really changed their mind and someone who is just pretending so they can gain support. Always research peoples' past claims and decide for yourself if they've had a real change of heart or not.

Another big red flag is when people promise you the moon, but fail to provide you with any instructions to actually get there. In other words, many people might claim that they can get your kids back from CPS, but when the time comes, they can't deliver on these promises. They may be unable to explain their plan for getting your child back simply because they don't really have one, and they are just stringing you along for your money. Look for people who can provide you with clear, actionable advice, and who have a good track record of successfully bringing kids home. At the end of the day, who would you trust more: someone who has never brought a kid back to their parents successfully, or someone who has returned 90 kids and counting?

Additionally, be wary of anyone who quickly tries to turn themselves into a figurehead while undermining the power of the people. Some will try to pull power away from the people and toward themselves. This is a good sign that they don't truly care about empowering everyone else in the movement, but instead they're only here to line their pockets. Be cautious of getting swept up by big-name people who claim to join the movement unless they seem like they're genuinely interested in helping everyone, not just themselves.

Battles With Big Names

The affidavit movement has already seen several attempted infiltrators as it has grown more powerful and gained recognition by bigger names. One such infiltrator is Professor David Clements, who has repeatedly tried to redirect the movement and steal it for his own gain. Clements serves as a reminder that not everyone who claims to share the values of the group actually does. Many people in politics are willing to say no to mask mandates and shutdowns, like Clements did, but this doesn't mean they are willing to work toward empowering the people with affidavits. Luckily, those who were paying attention noticed the warning signs, and identified Clements as an infiltrator.

Previously, Clements has repeatedly argued against the use of affidavits. He has claimed that they are essentially useless and that they don't help people get their kids back or fight back against other forms of government corruption like fraudulent elections, even in spite of clear evidence to the contrary. However, just a handful of months later, Clements spoke at the Mike Lindell symposium claiming to be fully in favor of affidavits. For one, this showcases a track record that isn't in line with his current claims. While some vocal critics do change their minds, given Clements' attempts to make the movement about himself and turn himself into its figurehead by taking credit for the affidavit movement at the Lindell symposium, it was clear that this wasn't a genuine change in opinion. Instead, it was primarily a vanity project that directed people away from the real proponents of the movement, David and Josh, and took the focus off the power of the people.

Another tip-off is that Clements repeatedly made promises with no solutions of his own. He did not give people the education and tools they needed to work toward change themselves. He repeatedly referred to David and Josh as grifters because they charge a small fee for their services and tried to expel them from the movement. He even went so far as to shun people who claimed to benefit from David and Josh's advice, removing them from chat rooms and barring them from the conversation. Despite this, he failed to show the people what they could do with affidavits, and was more than interested in making millions off the people through donations to add to his already considerable wealth. He brought no solutions of his own to the table, only repeating the advice of the people he had denounced.

In many cases, Clements made claims that were provably false, which served to get the whole movement labeled as a bunch of conspiracy theorists and harmed public image. Joe Oltmann, founder of Faith, Education, Commerce

United (FEC United) launched a fundraiser for Clements after the Professor got in hot water at his job for defying mask mandates. However, the fundraiser made the false claim that "Clements was 'fired for standing up' though he was actually on paid leave, and later revised to claim he was 'being fired,' writing that the termination was 'a forgone conclusion'" (D'Ammassa, 2021, para. 17). Clements was happy to have people send him their money when he was still collecting a check from work and truly did not need the support. This situation led many news outlets to call not just Clements but the whole movement a bunch of conspiracy theorists and liars, making the movement seem like a joke. In other words, Clements and his cohorts were offering little to no advice on how to use affidavits effectively while trying to take your money under the pretense of a lie. When people who are not part of the movement see these lies, they are more likely to dismiss the power of affidavits, and they may even discredit the idea that there is corruption in CPS and in other branches of the government as well. This interferes with the movement's goal of educating as many people as possible, making the people suffer for Clements' actions.

At the end of the day, big-name people who try to turn themselves into the face of the movement are no good for the American people. They are far from harmless; they directly interfere with the mission of the movement by claiming power and control for themselves rather than giving it back to the people. The movement does not need their support to succeed, so keep an eye out for people who would take your money and give you nothing of value in return.

Chapter 8

Have Faith

"I have lived, Sir, a long time, and the longer I live, the more convincing proofs I see of this truth - that God governs in the affairs of men."

Benjamin Franklin

In times of darkness, one of the most important things you can do is to have faith in God. Know that you do not go into any battle alone. The Lord is your shepherd, and he shall guide you to victory, even when you are facing down the greatest evils.

From the very beginning, both David and Josh felt called by God to empower the people. Their very meeting itself seemed like an act of God, as a mutual friend brought them together so they could learn how they could help each other in their battles. Since then, God has only made Himself more present in their work, helping them to achieve what would otherwise be impossible and reinforcing their convictions with faith. During a time when serious corruption and darkness threatens the future of the nation, it is only through God that average people can stand up and make a difference, fighting for what they believe in because they know that it's the right thing to do.

God's Guidance

God has been a consistent part of both David and Josh's lives in meaningful ways. For David, God is part of his relationship with his father. Previously, David's father was a gangster who was feared in the streets. He could have continued down that path of violence and crime, but after finding God, he was led away from it all. He focused on his family, and he helped teach David what he knows about what it means to do good in the world. For Josh, God's influence can be easily traced back through his ancestry, all the way back to the biblical figures of Solomon and David. For these two men to be brought together during a time of crisis, it seems clear that it can only be the will of God. After all, as it says in the Bible, "Learn to do good; seek justice, rebuke the oppressor; defend the fatherless, plead for the widow" (King

James Bible, Isaiah 1:17). When David and Josh are educating the people and empowering them through affidavits, they are doing exactly this, following God's teachings.

It should also come as no surprise that so many faithful people have joined the movement. Not everyone who supports the idea of rooting out corruption considers themselves faithful, but when you lack faith, it is much easier to be tempted to a life of sin. Meanwhile, many of the most significant and vocal supporters of the movement have been highly faithful, and after hearing the truth, they have done their part to support David and Josh's efforts. In other words, the faithful have heard the call to action, and they responded simply because it was the right thing to do. Meanwhile, those who have rejected God's teachings can be found everywhere on the political left, and often within the corrupt systems that increase the amount of evil in the world.

Good Versus Evil

The battle currently being waged within our country isn't just about politics. It isn't simply left versus right, or blue versus red. Similarly, the affidavit movement isn't just about CPS, mask mandates, vaccinations, elections, or other worldly issues. These are all symptoms of the problem, but they are not the root cause. Instead, this battle is really about good versus evil, and seeing who will respond to God's call to take action on the side of good, and who will allow evil to win.

If the past few years have taught the American public anything, it is that it is incredibly easy for evil to find a foothold in the world if no good people stand up and oppose it. If no one is here to call out evil deeds that infringe upon God-given rights as granted to the people by the U.S. Constitution, then this corruption will continue to grow and get worse over time. Those who would see this corruption take root are the truest source of evil in the modern world.

In June of 2020, Archbishop Carlo Maria Viganò released an open letter to President Trump speaking on the ways evil has manifested in the modern world. In the letter, he speaks of "those who serve themselves, who do not hold any moral principles, who want to demolish the family and the nation" fighting against the good and the just. Viganò refers to these people as "the children of darkness – whom we may easily identify with the deep state which [President Trump] wisely opposes and which is fiercely waging war against [him] in these days" (Viganò, 2020, para. 2-3). When the people take action against the deep state, they are taking action against the evils of the world and the children of darkness who would otherwise see the people suffer.

From Archbishop Viganò's description, it is clear which side of the current conflict represents good and which represents evil. Evil comes from those people in power who choose to wield their power with cruelty and for their own personal gain. The wicked are government officials and other influential people who work against God's wishes to increase the amount of evil in the world. They create corruption and profit off of the suffering of families and the American people. These people act like what they are doing is justified, but they are really working with sinister plans to destroy the nation and create a new world order. However, there is no reason to give up hope, because for as many evil people as there are in the world, there are far more good people who want to oppose evil in all its forms. The righteous American citizens are "those who, although they have a thousand defects and weaknesses, are motivated by the desire to do good, to be honest, to raise a family, to engage in work, to give prosperity to their homeland, to help the needy, and, in obedience to the Law of God, to merit the Kingdom of Heaven" (Viganò, 2020, para. 2). When those on the side of good work together, do not give up hope, and rely on their faith to see them through, they can accomplish a great deal with God's blessings.

God's Blessings

For as long as Josh and David have been working to teach the people about affidavits and make a positive change in their communities, they have also noticed that God has been looking out for them every step of the way. After all, the task they are undertaking is difficult, and some would even say impossible. For two average Joe's to stand against some of the most corrupt big names in politics and still achieve victory after victory is practically unthinkable if they were working alone. Of course, they were never really alone. They knew they had God on their side, because otherwise, they could never have accomplished all the things they had done. Josh wouldn't have been able to help so many business owners reopen during shutdowns. David wouldn't have been able to return so many kids to their families. They wouldn't have gotten access to so much hidden information, nor would they have had the chance to meet up with allies who supported their cause. Every instance of good fortune in spite of the odds stacked against them only reinforced their belief that God was and continues to be on their side.

Remember the Bible's Teachings

Through God, the people are empowered. Think of the story of David and Goliath, which is almost exactly mirrored in the modern day. The deep state and its allies are Goliath. They have all the power, all the control, and all the resources to protect themselves. They seem like a towering giant, impossible for an average person to take down. But the biblical David, whose size was a fraction of Goliath's and who seemed like he would surely lose, had an ace up his sleeve:

God. David had faith in the Lord, and he knew that standing up to Goliath was the right thing to do. Without armor or a sword, armed with only stones and a slingshot, David was able to beat Goliath, all because the Lord protected him, and because he placed his faith in God. When American citizens are up against the government, it can feel like fighting Goliath. Things may seem hopeless, but remember that with God on your side, you can face even the toughest challenges.

Education and cooperation are the hidden tools for success. This, too, is part of the Bible, which teaches us to band together with our fellow man. In the book of Genesis, the Bible states, "And the Lord said, Behold, the people is one, and they have all one language; and this they begin to do: and now nothing will be restrained from them, which they have imagined to do" (King James Bible, Genesis 11:6). This passage means that when the people come together to work toward the common good, and when thousands of people are sending in affidavits and demanding the government work for them as is their right granted by the Constitution, there is nothing they cannot accomplish. Put your faith in God, and you will never falter on the path to defeating evil.

Conclusion

"If we ever forget that we are One Nation Under God, then we will be a nation gone under."

Ronald Reagan

On January 16, 1919, the 18th Amendment was written into law. This amendment began the prohibition era, banning the import and export of alcohol in America. This law was deeply unpopular and only became more hated as time went on. Soon, the people decided they'd had enough. On December 5, 1933, the 21st Amendment was passed, repealing the 18th Amendment and ending prohibition at the will of the people. What did it take to make this change? Did millions of people have to petition their governments and barter away their first-born children to have their voices heard? No, in fact, it took just 180,000 people across the country, average citizens, notifying the government of their displeasure with the law to get an unconstitutional Amendment removed. The people exercised their right to do what they wanted within their own private property, and with just a small fraction of the population working together, they saw results. If just 180,000 people could have this significant of an impact, imagine what the millions of people across the nation who are watching videos and being informed about the power of affidavits can do when they take action.

The American people are asserting their rights and taking back power more and more every day. Dozens of states are launching their own investigations into election fraud, led by the people. Hundreds of families are taking CPS to task for their unconstitutional practices. Thousands of concerned citizens and business owners are fighting back against COVID-19 quarantine mandates. Millions of people are learning, perhaps for the first time, that they have more power than they thought, and that the government was created to carry out their will.

The truth is that you don't need to be able to attend law school to learn about your rights. You don't have to pass the bar exam, and you certainly don't need to be one of the political elite to enact real change. You can educate yourself and take direct action. Start by reading your state Constitution, especially the Bill of Rights that shows what the government can and can't do. Watch videos posted by David and other patriots looking to get the word out about affidavits and expose corruption in all its forms. Get involved and engaged. People all across America are waking up to the idea that the future of the nation is in their hands, and it's time to make a decision about what you are going to do with that power.

SAVING AMERICA

Ask yourself: if not now, then when? When will you stand up for your rights? Will you wait until things get worse? Will you leave your children and grandchildren a world where corruption runs rampant and no one is prepared to take action against it? Or will you choose to stand up for the rights of the people against those who would seek to abuse the power of their government stations? If you are going to defend your rights, the time to do so is today, right now. **It is only through action that you can help save America.**

Photo Gallery

CONTACT PAGE

If you need further assistance moving your business into the Private as a Private Membership Association please contact David or Josh. They also offer monthly Webinars (via WeConnect Real Law Telegram group) to teach people their constitutional rights and how to harness the powers given to us by our Founding Fathers.

barnettforaz.com
@barnettforaz - Twitter/Instagram
Barnett for Congress - Telegram
Josh Barnett for Congress- Facebook
Josh Barnett for US Congress - YouTube
contact@barnettforaz.com

WeConnect Real Law - Telegram
DaveCaresForYou - YouTube
@DaveCaresforYou - Telegram
restoremyrepublic.com

https://www.davecaresforyou.shop/

Made in the USA
Monee, IL
23 November 2021